Confucian China and Its Modern Fate

VOLUME TWO
The Problem of Monarchical Decay

Joseph R. Levenson

CONFUCIAN CHINA
AND ITS
MODERN FATE

VOLUME TWO

The Problem of Monarchical Decay

University of California Press

BERKELEY AND LOS ANGELES 1964

University of California Press
Berkeley and Los Angeles
California
© *Joseph R. Levenson 1964*
Printed in Great Britain

Preface

'THE Problem of Monarchical Decay' is the second volume of *Confucian China and Its Modern Fate*, which began with 'The Problem of Intellectual Continuity'. The work concludes in a third volume, 'The Problem of Historical Significance'.

It is mainly novelists, I suppose, who have brought out works meant to be integral, with a central core of characters and an over-arching design, though offered in several volumes 'complete in themselves'. I have in mind not so much the *roman fleuve*, which may take a family, for example, down through the years, but the broad panoramas, the novels of shifting context, where the same characters, at the same time, appear in different lights and situations. At least some historical themes, I think, can be treated like that. Some, indeed, demand it. A theme like 'Confucian China and its modern fate', if it is not to seem, under such a title, just a bit of Wagnerian pastiche, windy and portentous, has to be scored more than once.

The present book, then, follows on 'The Problem of Intellectual Continuity', but not in the usual chronological way, like 'The War Years' after 'The Prairie Years'. The contents of the volumes run parallel in time, not consecutively. Each volume should have an internal wholeness, while the set, I hope, will make a total effect itself. Certain themes which in one volume receive only limited treatment, appropriate to the part they play in developing a certain train of thought, are treated extensively elsewhere, as befits another context. Yet, the different contexts for the single theme, while separated for the purpose of exposition, should strike the reader of the whole work as mutually reinforcing.

For example, the anti-Confucian Taiping Rebellion

(1850–64) is touched on rather glancingly in Volume One, mainly as a foil to the Confucian syncretisms of the anti-Taiping Tseng Kuo-fan, and as a factor in the problem of the social implications of Christian proselytism, and as an element in a new tradition set in opposition to The Tradition. But in Volume Two it reappears, in a detailed discussion of the Taiping clash with the Confucian conception of monarchy. And this discussion is part of a general exploration of the tension between monarchy and bureaucracy in Confucian China; the significance of that tension for the very definition of Confucian China; and the reasons for the relaxation of that tension and the reduction of Confucianism to vestigial status.

This is an 'institutional' counterpart of the 'intellectual' explanation in Volume One. In Volume One, I posed the problem of Confucian China's modern fate in intellectual terms: how and why, during so much of Chinese history, have new ideas had to face tests of compatibility with received tradition, while in more recent times tradition has had to face tests of compatibility with independently persuasive new ideas? In Volume Two, I pose the problem—the *same* problem—in institutional terms: how and why have monarchy and bureaucracy been so intimately involved in the Confucian view of culture that abolition of the first, and transformation of the second, have rendered partisans of the third more *traditionalistic* than *traditional*?

'Confucianism' is an amorphous term. I have taken it seriously, and and my 'Confucian China' is not just a carelessly chosen loose equivalent of 'traditional China'. Of course, there was more to China, much more, than Confucianism. In Volume One, I gave some attention to the Buddhist side of things, and, in the present volume, to Legalism—not that these are all. Yet, the aim is not just to present a many-sided picture of China; it is still necessary, I think, to lean to one side. Certainly we should realize that a thoroughly Confucian China is an unhistorical abstraction. But we should retain the Confucian abstraction in our minds, instead of dismissing it under the weight of evidence of Legalist qualification. We have to retain it in our minds just because out there, in history, the abstraction is surely blurred. Then we can ask, what blurs it? If Confucius was revered as the Chinese sage (to put it at its simplest), what interfered with his influence? If a moving body ought to continue to move with its first speed and direction, what forces slow it down and redirect it?

Confucianism, then, was never alone in the Chinese universe. But it did not simply yield room to other bodies of thought and institutions. They interacted, in a system with a history. One way to unravel the history is to check the 'revisionist' ardour, retain the concept 'Confucian China' in spite of the prominence of other strains, and see how the latter bring historical tensions to the otherwise pure (or unhistorical) Confucian ideas and offices.

Confucianism, besides sharing space, in a system, had a place in time, in a history. How large a place may we allot it? There can be just as much a question of the length of its existence as of the breadth. How can a book which purports to be about 'Confucian China' spend many pages on the nineteenth century, when Confucius lived about twenty-five centuries earlier?

This is a constructive question, in that it warns, rightly, against smearing the Chinese eras together. Individualities must be respected and the sense of change never dulled. But the question may be obstructive, too, if it puts a case for nominalism. The very truth which the question vindicates, that China has a history, would be obscured by the suggestion that discrete atoms fill it. There was not just one Confucianism over twenty-five hundred years; but there was not just one Confucianism, a school in the age of the 'Warring States'. There have been, instead, Confucianisms—plural, changing, but still with some real persistence. I have tried in this book to give full weight to process, not stasis, and to show what *happened to* Confucianism. But Confucianism was a feature of many landscapes in time, and I have felt it relevant at many moments to refer to the glimpses in many others.

Indeed, the question of generality does not stop there. Along with lines stretching down between such eras as Han, Sung, Ming, and Ch'ing, the lines go out to France, Germany, Russia, and Japan, among others. Here, too, I have meant not to force identities but to recognize relevancies. These are comparisons, not analogies, and they seem to me to throw light not only on Chinese history but on the purpose of history-writing, on this subject, in this day.

From at least the late nineteenth century, men in all parts of the world have looked, with hope or alarm but with more and more conviction, to an impending unification of the world. This has provided the theme for much profound speculation and many banalities. People everywhere wonder about the cultural implications of a universal science and technology, and various intellectual imperatives have been suggested. Some speak of the need to construct a culture out of selected values from particular histories, so that a cultural esperanto will accord with the new technological universe. Others speak rather of essentially parallel histories, whose cultural destinations will be essentially the same. However, I do not consider that history can ever be made in the first way, as though by cultural selection boards, taking the best from East and West for a nice synthetic balance (see Volume One); and I do not think it has been made in the second way, down some universal paradigm, Marxist or Toynbeean or any other.

As a matter of fact, just such assumptions as these are in the record I wish to study in *Confucian China*. But while I study them as historical subjects that need explaining, not as objectively valid explanations themselves of the course that history takes, I share something of the premise behind them. For something is emerging that really can be called world history, not just the sum of histories of separate civilizations. Historians of China can help to make this history as they write of the past. Far removed from any fact or fancy of cultural 'aggression' or cultural apologetics, an historian, by bringing China into a universal world of discourse, helps to unify the world on more than a technological level. There should be no question of contriving syntheses or of warping

Chinese history to fit some western model. Instead, a world
is made when an understanding of Chinese history, without
violence to its integrity and individuality, and an understanding of western history reinforce each other. They belong
together not because they reproduce each other (which is
false), and not because economic expansion or political em-
broilments or intellectual influences bring them into touch
(though this is true), but because minds of observers can
transpose the problems (not, transplant the problems) of one
into the other.

Chinese bureaucracy is not analogous to Prussian, but it is
comparable (see Volume Two). When Burckhardt too
hastily believed the rumour of the burning of the Louvre by
the Communards, he could have no notion of an Imperial
Palace Museum; but one who thinks of this museum in
Peking and the fall of Chinese principalities and powers must
think of Burckhardt's attitude, for the issue of revolution and
culture, 'high' and otherwise, is a universal issue (see Volume
Three). And Chinese history, then, should be studied not just
for exotic appeal or importance to western strategy. It should
be studied because—without making the same designs—it can
be seen to make sense in the same world of discourse in which
we try to make sense of the West. If we can make this kind of
sense, perhaps we help to make this kind of world. The act of
writing history is an historic act itself.

Like its predecessor, this volume owes a very great deal to
conferences held under the auspices of the Committee for
Chinese Thought of the Association for Asian Studies. I am
very grateful to Arthur F. Wright, the chairman of the
committee and of its conferences on Confucianism, and to all
the participants, many of whose names will be found in the
text or in the footnotes. Their scholarship and penetrating
comments have been indispensable, though they are free of
responsibility for my uses and abuses. Some of the material,
too, was given a hearing at the 'Conference on Political
Power in Traditional China', 1959, under the direction of
John K. Fairbank. I am delighted to thank him again, as

PREFACE

I have done, or should have done, so many times for so many things since 1939. Among colleagues and students at the University of California, Franz Schurmann and Pow-key Sohn have been especially generous with their help on this volume. My wife, to whom the first volume was dedicated, has gone over the manuscript with a stabbing blue pencil. She was too kind to sharpen it as fine as she might have liked, but I am grateful to her for clearing out at least some of the faults of style.

A fellowship at the Center for Advanced Study in the Behavioral Sciences at Palo Alto, a Guggenheim fellowship for a year at St. Antony's College and the Oriental Institute, Oxford, and the Center for Chinese Studies at the University of California, Berkeley, have all contributed enormously to the research, discussion, and writing which have gone into this book. It seems rather a mini-mouse from such a mountain of support, but I hope the directors and foundations concerned will accept this expression of deep appreciation.

Parts of the book in different form have been published in *Confucianism in Action*, ed. David S. Nivison and Arthur F. Wright (Stanford, 1959), and in *Comparative Studies in Society and History*. I wish to thank the publishers and editors for permission to use the material here.

J. R. L.

Contents

CONTENTS

Part Three: The Break in the Line of Tension

CONTENTS

Part Four: The Vestige of Suggestiveness: Confucianism and Monarchy at the Last (II)

xiii

Part One

THE SUGGESTIVENESS OF VESTIGES: CONFUCIANISM AND MONARCHY AT THE LAST (I)

Hommes de l'avenir souvenez-vous de moi
Je vivais a l'époque ou finissaient les rois . . .

APOLLINAIRE, *Alcools*

CHAPTER I

The Draining of the
Monarchical Mystique

I. THE HUNG-HSIEN EMPEROR AS A COMIC TYPE

IN 1914 Yüan Shih-k'ai, trying to be the strong man not by
muscle alone, but by mystique, contrived a bit of ceremonial. He still called his state the Min-kuo, the Republic,
and he still called himself a president, not an emperor, but he
meant to be a president with quite remarkable staying powers,
and he looked for some awe to reinforce his political arrangements. Accordingly, he embellished his presidential election
law (which was frankly designed as a guarantee that Yüan
would succeed himself and succeed himself) with a ritualistic
rigmarole to add a touch of suspense—three names, the
president's private and secret choices, put in a gold box kept
in a stone house in the presidential palace enclosure, the
president with the one key to the gold box, the president and
two of his appointees with the three keys to the stone house,
the dramatic disclosure to a safe electoral college of the three
names three days before the election, the thoughtful addition
of the president's name to his roster of tame candidates, etc.[1]
It was a cunning plan.

However, he never used it. His real aim was to invoke a
sanctity, not to create one, and the comical complexity of his
'republican' devices—his mummery for presidents and his
plethora of schemes for treadmill rounds of provisional
parliaments and provisional constitutions—were better made
to mock the Republic than to make it seem legitimate. Total

discredit of the Republic was a preamble; then, the body of the tale might be a new dynastic history. Yüan's conversation, it was commonly noted, kept turning to the question of 'the success of the Republic'. He put it to all provincial officials when they came to Peking.[2] The implication was plain: they were free, more than free, to denigrate the Republic. Yüan, though its chief executive, would surely take no offence.

Yet, when Yüan finally inaugurated the Hung-hsien reign on January 1, 1916, the parody of a republic yielded (for just a few months) to only a parody of the empire. And this was perhaps inevitable, the result not of some failure of dignity in Yüan himself, but of a condition of modern Chinese history in the large: the vitiation of old conventions, an invincible staleness which all the futilities of the republican alternative, obvious though they were, could not dispel. Goethe's Faust had seen his emperor's court as a world of masks for emptiness, and court and carnival as one.[3] And the question that needs to be asked about Yüan's imperial masquerade, about all the vestigial monarchism in the Chinese Republican era, is the question that Mann's Faust-as-the-artist put to himself: 'Why does almost everything seem to me like its own parody? Why must I think that almost all, no, all the methods and conventions of art today are good for parody only?'[4]

The imperial office in 1916 could not be taken seriously, because the Republic of 1912, while a failure, was not a mistake. Its failure lay in its social meaninglessness; the revolution seemed to have had no substance. As the great Lu Hsün (1881–1936) mordantly remarked of the trivial changings of the guard at the bureaucrats' yamens: '. . . Those who wore cotton clothing when they came to serve in his office had changed into fur gowns within ten days, although the weather was not yet cold.'[5]

But the Republic, however insubstantial, did have meaning as a symbol: by its mere existence after thousands of years of monarchy, it offered licence to new thought, the solvent of Chinese pieties. Yüan Shih-k'ai, by trying to make himself stick as emperor, asserted in effect that no political revolution had occurred in 1911 and 1912, only, at most, a traditional rebellion between dynastic periods. However, his monarchism, in defiance of this interpretation, was compromised by a revolution which *was* occurring, the intellectual revolution. When the Republic, devoid of social achievement though it may have been, shameless political fake though it may have seemed, nevertheless stood for something—iconoclasm—its rival, monarchy, had to stand for something, too (and something, as we shall see, fatally equivocal): traditionalism.

Much of Yüan's support, even during his imperial episode, was not monarchical in principle. He had his personal followers, playing parts in factional struggle, and many of them said yes to monarchy because Yüan wanted it, not because they did. A few men with their private hopes invested in Yüan, and others even with confidence in him, would have followed him anywhere. But he needed more than these companions in his quest for imperial honours. Not Yüan Shih-k'ai but Chinese Empire had to be the cause, and anti-Republican feeling, in the nature of the times, was tied in with tradition.

At first, the only monarchism visible after the revolution was a faint rally for the fallen house, the Ch'ing. There remains an impression that Yüan was mildly indulgent to this campaign; perhaps it would soften up the public for his own.[6] The latter began, it appears, in 1913, when he set up a bureau for a Ch'ing Dynastic History. This respectable patronage of scholarship did double duty politically. It showed Yüan in the old monarchical vein, and it implied a last quietus on the Ch'ing. (At the high point of his imperial drive, Yüan gave Chao Erh-sun, the principal drafter of the History, a new court title as one of the 'four Friends of Sungshan'.)[7]

In November 1914 Yüan elicited a petition with two agreeable features, a plea for a strict ban on the Ch'ing interest, and a list of flaws in the Republic. A somewhat earlier petition had been just as militant on the flaws, but quixotically urged Yüan to restore the Manchu emperor and be his minister. He answered both with an 'edict of chastisement of the restoration movement'.[8] And on December 23, 1914, when Yüan publicly reinstituted the worship of Heaven, he changed the

5

signature on the prayer-tablet from the Ch'ing's *Tzu-ch'en* ('Your son and subject') to 'Yüan Shih-k'ai representing the citizens of the Chinese Republic'.[9] Correctly republican, no doubt—but reminiscent of an older form. He would rather the rite than the presidency. He was still not ready to perform the ceremony in his own imperial name, but he was ready enough for the ceremony, hoping to ease himself eventually from one traditional role up to another.

Yüan made gentle demurrers at the offer of the throne in early December 1915 ('Our sage-master emerged with destiny . . . the people submit to your virtue, the whole nation is of one mind . . .' pronounced his Council of State, humbly petitioning that he 'graciously indulge the feelings of the people').[10] He discreetly extracted a formal blessing from the Ch'ing ex-emperor ('In accordance with the command of the Ch'ing emperor: with regard to changing the form of state and raising the president to imperial honours, the Ch'ing royal house deeply approves').[11] And in striking these poses he conformed to the pattern of *shan-jang*, cession and seemly initial rejection, which derived from the *Shu-ching* (Book of History) lore of Yao and Shun. When modesty ceased to forbid him, Yüan accepted the offer ('For the empire's rises and falls the very commoner has responsibility; shall my love of country lag behind others?')[12]—in Chinese phrases of classical cadence and in part, at least, in direct echo of the seventeenth century's Ku Yen-wu.[13] The republican bureaucracy's *ch'eng* ('submit' [a document]) gave way to the grand old *tsou* ('memorialize'); the ancient monarchical *ch'en*, for 'official' (the Ch'ing mark of Confucian distinction between the Chinese official and the Manchu *nu*, or 'slave'), supplanted the current *kuan* in the bureaucratic nomenclature.[14] And on the last day of 1915, when the next year was proclaimed as Hung-hsien 1, Yüan gave to the *Yen sheng kung*, the 'Holy Duke', K'ung Ling-i, direct descendant of Confucius, the brevet rank of *chün-wang*, a feudal title of Han devising and long in imperial use.[15] In these and a hundred other ways old legitimacies were solicited for Yüan Shih-k'ai. But when the Emperor Yüan was traditionalistic, as he had to be, he ran through an emperor's lines, he followed the ancient stage directions, but he was not (nor could anyone else then be) an authentic, traditional emperor.

2. LATE CH'ING: CONFUCIANISM REDEFINED AS THE COUNTER TO MODERN THOUGHT

Actually, monarchy was lost when the Manchu dynasty, the Ch'ing, was forced to improvise after the Boxer débâcle of 1900, and traditionalistic monarchy, which was untraditional, was preordained for Yüan Shih-k'ai by his Ch'ing dynastic predecessors. For the Ch'ing were in a hopeless dilemma in their last decade. Immobility was impossible, something had to be done to save the State. The Boxer expedients, magic and xenophobia, could surely never be tried again. Science and social renewal insistently commended themselves. There had to be modernization, or the Ch'ing would never escape the blame for continuing Chinese disasters.

Yet, their sponsorship of modernization, the abandonment of traditional Chinese ways, would end their only claim, as an ethnically foreign people, to legitimacy as Chinese rulers. This legitimacy a pre-nationalistic 'culturalism' had once accorded them, since the Manchus had generally supported the Chinese great tradition. But Chinese nationalism, necessarily spreading as Chinese culture changed (see Volume One), found a foreign conquest, old or new, inadmissible, and the Manchu conquest-dynasty entirely illegitimate. In short, in their last decade the Ch'ing had a discouraging choice. They might go down in a traditional way, out of simple cyclical weakness in a world of outer pressures and inner strains. They might go down as moderns, aspiring, at least, to strengthen China, strengthen their hold, and thereby extend their title to the traditional mandate, but running afoul of the nationalism which modern, foreign strengthening methods entailed. Quite naturally, no clear-cut choice was made. Given a situation in which the best of both worlds was in another light the worst, they tried to be modern enough to defend their traditional status, and traditional enough to take the curse off their modernism.

That is why the 'Manchu Reform Movement' in the early

nineteen-hundreds was undertaken in the *t'i-yung* spirit, seductive but self-defeating (see Volume One): Chinese learning should be for 'essence', western learning for 'utility'. The western learning was supposed to strengthen China materially, thus keeping Ch'ing from the typical end of dynasties when China was enfeebled. The Chinese learning was supposed to reconfirm the Manchus' credentials, by preserving traditional values essentially unimpaired, and still the focus of loyalty, so that Manchus could still be Manchus and yet be identified with China. But if the *t'i*, the essence, could really not be saved, Manchus were endangered, even more than the Chinese *t'i* addicts. Chinese advocates of a *t'i-yung* programme might prove wrong in their expectations, and yet their heirs would go on being Chinese, though with a new intellectual content to their lives. But Manchus, once their Confucian ticket of admission became invalid, could go on being Chinese only by assimilation, ethnic disappearance. At most they would survive rather as museum-pieces, a few visible remnants, aristocratic and anachronistic, exquisitely formed by the high Chinese culture of an age that was not their own.

Thus, there was something ominous about the Ch'ing's new educational policies, beginning in 1901. They led to actions perhaps nationally constructive, but dynastically destructive (just as inaction would have been). In part it was simply a problem of allocation of scarce resources. The new learning was supposed to supplement the old, but right at the start it began to look like substitution instead. Where were the new schools coming from? An edict of September 14, 1901, ordained that provincial *shu-yüan*, Confucian academies, be made into new-style institutions of higher learning.[16] The very physical premises of *t'i*, that is, were being invaded by *yung*. And this reflected an intellectual trend, the shortening of perimeter around the unimpeachable essence. From the hint in the eighteen-forties of a readiness to yield military technology to a world of western practice, more and more of what once was Chinese essence had been peeled off, in efforts to guard a deeper core.

The less that remained of the traditional core, the more its character as substance, eternally underlying mere function, had to be insisted on. No memorial about new schools, study abroad, the cultivation of modern talents could be complete without its mention of the Four Books and the Five Classics, the Histories, the filial and other established virtues, as the indispensable first concerns; *then* one could steep the mind in western learning.[17] And so one finds the anomalies of a 1906 decree about the new educational system—a sharp departure from the examination system (abolished the year before), which was centuries old and of incalculable significance for the traditional social order and cultural values. The new education was to have military spirit, industrial spirit, and public spirit generally among its main objectives—so much for the leanings to modernism—and loyalty to the Emperor and reverence for Confucius as vital bequests from the past. At the same time, as if to reinforce the latter strain, the Ch'ing decreed that sacrifices to Confucius be raised to the grade of *ta-ssu*, 'great sacrifices', the highest grade of three. Hitherto these spring and autumn ceremonies had been left to officials, but now the Emperor himself was to perform them in Peking.[18]

Yet, this Confucian zeal of the Manchus (always apparent in Ch'ing history as a means of their growing into China on some principle other than ethnic, and heightened, if anything, at the last) only intensified Confucianism to the point of exhaustion. For it was obviously being 'worked at' for a social purpose, as something to spoil the potentialities, which were anti-Manchu, of implicitly nationalistic modern thought. Sun Yat-sen's Chinese nationalists saw the logic of this modern Confucian commitment. 'Let Confucius not be an amulet for the Manchu,' Sun's Tokyo organ, *Min-pao*, intoned in 1907. 'The Tartar court, with the revolutionary tide rising in the new thought, thereupon makes the worship of Confucius a supreme sacrificial rite.'[19]

Thus, Confucianism was being deprived of almost its last intellectual substance, and left as mainly a symbol of resistance to revolution. When revolution came, it was clear that change in régime had powerfully furthered a change in mind. Classics and ceremonies fell widely into discard, while old Confucianists tried to rally in private organizations, reactionary in the fullest sense.[20] For Confucianists were only reacting to the tide of strange events; they were no longer the natural actors in a society of their own. When the Republic, justified by Sun Yat-sen as the 'latest thing' in a universal process of political improvement, opened the lid on the latest things in every other sphere, people with vested interests in the old régime, or simple nostalgia, clung fiercely and particularly to Confucianism, which was, after all, an early thing itself, and a glorifier of early things.

3. THE REPUBLIC: CONFUCIANISM AND MONARCHISM NARROWED AND INTERWOVEN

It was an attenuated Confucianism, then, more a sentiment than a teaching, which confronted republican scepticism about the value of the past, and which gravitated unerringly to any monarchical movement that seemed to have a chance. Prominent among the petitioners for monarchy in 1915 were the *K'ung-she*, Confucian societies, of Chihli and Honan.[21] In a broad generalization Yen Fu (1849–1921), dubbed at the time, though perhaps unfairly, one of Yüan's 'six *chün-tzu*' (sardonic analogy with the 'six martyrs' of 1898, Reformers sold by Yüan to the Empress Dowager),[22] revealed the new traditionalism's associations. As a conservative statement for that time and place, it was characteristically untraditional: 'Chinese honour the prince and venerate the ancient; westerners honour the people and venerate the modern.'[23]

What is untraditional here is the identification of Chinese monarchism with intellectual traditionalism pure and simple. This was a change from the live imperial days, when the monarchy, or its centralizing agents, often strained against the conservatism of the bureaucratic intelligentsia; from their very beginnings the traditional Chinese bureaucratic and monarchical institutions had existed in a state of mutual and ambivalent attraction-repulsion (Part Two). What is characteristic here, in the contemporary context of Yen's untraditional assumption, is the air of conscious response to a serious foreign challenge, that of democratic thought and other intellectual novelty. The intellectually subversive revolutionary nationalists had injected the *min*, 'the people', into modern political consciousness, and the *min* (or their self-styled representatives) had not only ousted the old monarchy, but had forced their way into the new monarchical thinking —indeed, had made it new.

Wu T'ing-fan (1844–1922), Sun Yat-sen's representative in conversations with the Ch'ing camp in late 1911, made a statement on December 20 to the effect that the new republican government would be based on *jen-min i-chih*, the people's 'will'.[24] On February 1, 1912, the dynasty itself ordered Yüan, its last agent, to come to terms with the revolutionary *min-chün*, 'people's army': 'The people's will has become clear . . .' And in the first edict of abdication, on February 12, came the sad renunciation: 'By the indications of men's minds the mandate of Heaven is known.'[25] Here was the contradiction of the principle of heavenly selection, to which popular control and ratification were essentially irrelevant.

In the ensuing contradiction of republicanism, 'the people' could not be exorcized from the monarchists' apologies. Sometimes the 'people's will' was retained, in the Bonapartist sense, as in Yüan's amusingly hyper-successful plebiscite for monarchy in the fall of 1915; more often, the Chinese people's 'spirit', not its will, was emphasized as the guarantor of the imperial institution. The famous memorandum along these lines by Professor Goodnow, Yüan's American adviser, was issued to the Press in August 1915. It inspired or released a flood of Chinese writings on *kuo-t'i* and *kuo-ts'ui* and *kuo-ch'ing*, the people's proper form of state, the national 'spirit' or temperament, which implied not that this Chinese republic was puerile but that no Chinese republic was possible, that monarchism was inexpungeable from the Chinese people's spirit.

(a) The 'people's will'

Why must the idea of 'the people' as source of political authority be seen as essentially modern in China, and appropriate enough, therefore, to an untraditional republic,

but not to a monarchy needing to trade on authentic traditional lineage? After all, there have been plenty of suggestions
in the last half-century or so that western democratic theory
was anticipated in ancient China; there, the imperial idea
(or so it is alleged) demanded the people's happiness as test
of fulfilment of the will of Heaven by the Son of Heaven.[26]
But such suggestions confuse the priorities in classical Chinese
thought. A modern appeal to 'the people' for validation
denies, not derives from, the old imperial sanctions.

To say that *vox populi* is *vox Dei* is not to define the latter
but to displace it. Here, in any literal sense, the 'voice of
God' has lost its power; rendered metaphorical, it only
underscores through historical tone the acknowledgement of
a new supreme authority. In imperial China the *T'ien-tzu*
held the *T'ien-ming* as long as he expressed the *T'ien-i*.[27]
Heaven's son, mandate, and will were unequivocally the
classical founts of supremacy, and the people's will, when it
was worked at all by Confucian thinkers into political theory,
was purely symbolic, not effective, in establishing legitimacy.
Heaven's hand could not be forced.[28]

In traditional monarchical theory, that is, popular discontent did not by itself invalidate an emperor's claims—nor,
by the same token, did popular approbation legitimize him.
Popular discontent was a *portent*, as a flood might be a portent,
of the loss of the mandate; it was a sign, perhaps, of the loss
of imperial virtue. But a flood was not to be greeted with
fatalistic acceptance. While an emperor should read the
signs aright, he still should try to check the flood. And just so,
the outbreak of a popular rebellion was no guarantee of its
success or of its Confucian acceptability (far from it). It might
be a portent, but it, too, should be and legitimately might be
resisted. For the famous 'right to rebel' was a contradiction in
terms. People rebelled not because they had any theoretical
legal right, but because actual legal arrangements left little
scope to their lives. Until they succeeded, rebels had no right,
and the people's will, if they claimed to express it, had to wait
on Heaven's choosing.

If he had the name, the 'rectified name', of Son of Heaven,
the ruler had the *te* which the Ju (Confucian) school thought

intrinsic to him—a *te* which was power on the outside and virtue, the *tao i hsing*, in his inner nature, a *te* which would bring no harm to the people's lives.[29] But popular satisfaction was one thing only in the classical political ideal: a sign of some higher ratification of the Emperor's legitimacy. It was another thing in the modern aura of secular democracy: the legitimizer itself.

And just as vestigial monarchy derived, allegedly, from the people's will, instead of simply according with it while reflecting Heaven's, so vestigial Confucianism took the people's will as its novel justification. 'If our parliamentarians really want to represent the people's will, then they cannot but establish Confucianism as the national religion,' wrote a petitioner in 1917, the year after 'Hung-hsien' and unpropitious for Confucian special pleaders. 'Catholics oppose the idea of a state religion,' he went on, 'but some three million Catholics are not the people's will.'[30] Mass identification with Confucianism, then, established by the evidence of history, was the ground of Confucian authority for this thinker and many others. It was the same sort of ground as Yüan had sought as the basis of his dynasty.

(b) *The 'people's spirit'*

But post-Ch'ing monarchism and Confucianism were linked more directly than that; it was not just that they both claimed identification with the people's will. The writer of this memorial for Confucianism (*not* a Confucian memorial), coming after Yüan's fiasco, had an embarrassed awareness of general opinion, which held Confucianism implicated in the discredited monarchical effort. It was hard to reconcile Confucianism with the symbolically modern Republic, but he did as well as he could. He admitted the charge of the Yüan affinity, dismissed it as a foible of Confucianists rather than a necessity of Confucianism, and suggested an act of oblivion. Christian churches, too, he pointed out, had launched prayers for Yüan's success. Christians, he alleged, were Yüan's loudest extollers, and took part in his government. Buddhists and Mohammedans repeatedly cheered him on. Yüan, he acknowledged, had fabricated a 'people's will' for his own monarchical purposes. But the genuine people's will was with Confucianism. Therefore, if Confucianism were established as the national religion of the Republic, it would prove itself indispensable for consolidating the State.[31]

In short, reasonably enough under the circumstances, this partisan was trying to free Confucianism from any necessary political tie. Of course, the effort to pry Confucius out of the royal box was already an old story in newly republican China. There was an apologist in 1912, for example (with a curious hint of limitation on the Sage he proclaimed eternal), who explained that Confucius, having been born in an age of monarchy, could have had no choice but to respect the institution.[32] Republics or monarchies were uncertain, but Confucianism was permanent while a Chinese people lived, for it was particularly (historically) a part of the Chinese people, its very spirit or essence. Every country has a form which is natural to it alone. Hence, 'Our country ought to establish Confucianism as the national religion . . . especially to protect the national essence.'[33]

It was this idea of Confucianism, its conception as national essence, that completed the ravages wrought by its Ch'ing defenders. Confucianism as 'essence', *t'i*, hopefully combined with 'utility', *yung*, had been a false solution to the problem of keeping alive the ancient wisdom. But when Confucianism slipped to *kuo-t'i*, *national* essence, this was worse than merely no solution to the problem of preservation—it was dissolution of the *t'i* to be preserved. As *t'i*, Confucianism was the essence of civilization, an absolute. As *kuo-t'i* or one of its synonyms, Confucianism was the essence of Chinese civilization, a complex of values (not absolute Value) in a world of historical relativism. A romantic conception of Confucianism as Chinese essence stripped Confucianism of *its* essence: a rationalistic assumption that the Way was the Way, no matter where or when, not just the particular Chinese way of life.

As early as 1905, soon after the abandonment of the examination system, we find an appeal to revere the Classics so as to preserve the national essence.[34] All the propaganda for Confucianism as a religion made the same particular point. Wherein lies the spirit, the soul of China? In the

Confucian *tao, hsüeh, chiao*—the Way, the learning, the doctrine or religion.[35] President Yüan Shih-k'ai wrangled over it with Sun's party, the Kuomintang, in the legislative session of 1913. Yüan wishing to establish Confucianism, the Kuomintang opposing it, they compromised. According to the 'Temple of Heaven' draft of a constitution, freedom of religion was not to be abridged, but for the national education the *tao* of Confucius was named as the basis of *hsiu-shen*, the inner cultivation of the person.[36]

Yüan soon slammed the door on the 'Temple of Heaven' draft, and, as his imperial ambitions grew, he made stronger statements on his side of the Confucian issue. Toward the end of 1914, for example, presidential mandates praised *tao* and *te*, the Confucian ethic, as the very root of government. Yüan emphasized that these were indelibly Chinese, confirmed by thousands of years of history, and that China must keep its national character, for every viable nation has its essence, a special spirit that forms it and preserves it.[37]

Where the quality of Confucian faith was less tinged with personal interest, outside Yüan's immediate circle, the religious Confucian movement had the same romantic feeling. That is, the Chinese people was urged to practise its own religion, Confucianism (Chinese, not universal, not proper to the West), on the ground that non-Chinese peoples, if well advised, were practising theirs (foreign, not universal, not proper to China). This committed Confucianists to non-Confucian thinking, a doctrine of separate but equal ultimate values. These men would not adopt a Christian *message* for China; they had to resist displacement of one universal world-view by another. But they could adopt a Christian *model* in a particularistic spirit, and preserve Confucius by seeing the world as a congeries of irreducible loyalties. Christians had cathedrals; then let Confucianists build a cathedral and start out, not on the road to Rome, but nevertheless on the road to a holy city—Ch'ü-fu, in Shantung, the birthplace of Confucius, which ought to be a pilgrimage place like Mecca or Jerusalem.[38] Christians dated by *Anno Domini*; then chih-sheng 2467 (from the birth-date of the Sage) stood for *Min-kuo* 5 or 1916.[39]

But why should 'national essence' Confucianism come in religious form? After all, not foreign missionaries now but Chinese secularists were making the really wounding assault on Confucianism. What defence should it be against these foes to stand off Christianity, by matching it? Yet, when Confucianists like K'ang Yu-wei (1858–1927) and his follower, Ch'en Huan-chang, deliberately courted religious comparisons, they were trying to reach the secular iconoclasts. For, as long as the adjective 'Confucian' was simply pinned on to Chinese culture, it was hard to escape the cultural critics in the harsh times of the early twentieth century. But if Confucianism was a church, like Christianity, then the modern progress of western states was no stick for belabouring Confucius. Western example proved that Church and State could coexist, and men could worship while enriching their society. As Christian religious bodies survived with science, just so (and only so), as a religious body, would Confucianism survive.

This was an effort, then, to dissociate Confucianism from Chinese material weakness. Sometimes the earlier Reformist argument, cool but not extinguished, was made again: Confucianism was the source of strength, and the West was strong where it came close to the message of the Analects, the Annals, Mencius—nourish the people, protect the people, teach the people.[40] But more characteristically for the Republican period, even the same writer, same text, would cordon off this wisdom in a church, so as to spare it imputations of failure, rather than claim for it social success. Why should Confucianism be compromised by Chinese weakness? Judaea fell, Christian imperial Rome fell, Catholic Spain and Portugal and Latin America, the Mohammedan countries, all were weak; yet their religions were not ruled out by their national incapacities.[41]

In this apology one sees the significant relativism of the post-Confucian Confucianist, the traditionalistic traditionalist. The faith is not a universal, but a matter of *mutatis mutandis*. Truth, forsooth—you have your religion, I have my religion. And all religions have a claim on life in their proper historical contexts. Confucianism certainly makes its claim in its own environment, China. 'The whole history of China is only the history of *K'ung-chiao*, the Confucian religion. We love China; therefore we love the *K'ung-chiao* . . . *K'ung-Chiao* is an interchangeable term for *Chung-kuo.*'[42] Or, in brief, from the father of them all: 'China's soul is in the *chiao* of Confucius.'[43]

More deeply than any merely strategic connection, K'ang Yu-wei felt this mystical connection between Confucius and China. It is true that he looked to his state religion to improve morality, since he believed that law and philosophy were not enough to restrain the wayward crowd.[44] Still, K'ang's candidate for state religion was specifically Chinese—not Christianity, for example, which might claim as well as Confucianism (or a little better) to endow men with a healthy sense of supernatural power. For it was the soul of China that interested K'ang, not the souls of individuals, irrespective of the cultures they were born to.

Now, the anti-Confucianists were especially exercised by this national essence-spirit-soul equation with Confucianism. One line of attack was to deny that Confucianism was any more 'Chinese' than the other currents of ancient thought.[45] But Ch'en Tu-hsiu (1880–1942), though he made that point, more forcefully simply swept away the idea of national essence. China should have what modern men required, and Confucianism (he wrote in 1916) was a fossil, fatal to vitality in the present.[46] When Confucian religionists tried to dissociate their creed from Chinese secular weakness, it was in answer to such attacks; indeed, they offered the *Church* Confucianism as a saving rock in the sea of material troubles.

Religion, they averred, was strength when all else failed, not the cause of failure itself. China should keep Confucianism, its very life for ages past, so suited to the people's hearts, because the nation, like a rudderless boat, would crack without it.[47] Confucianism was China's special nature; if stripped of it the nation would die, the people would not continue.[48] Jewish history was frequently cited as an inspiration to China, and Mexican history as a cautionary tale: the Jews, by preserving Judaism, had kept themselves alive when they were politically ruined, but the Mexicans, Hispanicized and weaned away from their own religion, were languishing in a travesty of a nation.[49] A nation that scuttled its historic religion prepared the way for its enemies. In a remarkable feat of kaleidoscoping, selection, and not very gallant aspersion on a lady of the theatre, K'ang observed that in the French Revolution the worship of a prostitute ('Goddess of Reason' in a public Deist charade) had been substituted for the worship of Christ; along came the 'hundred days' and the end.[50] When Norway split off from Sweden in 1905 (ran another expression of opinion) many changes were made in the constitution, but Lutheranism, long the state religion, remained so, as the link with the people's past. Moral: 'As the physical body without the spirit must die, so must the nation without a national religion.'[51] 'Other countries, in some numbers, have established national religions. Is there not still more reason for us to do likewise? For Confucianism is our religion by nature.'[52]

And so states may die for the lack of their own religions, and peoples may survive, though states die, if their religions are kept alive. This was another argument to extricate Confucianism from the modern plight of China (not quite the same argument as the one about religion and progress co-existing, so that Confucian *religion* was out of the way when the modernists came to arrest Confucian *culture*). For K'ang Yu-wei and his fellow thinkers, Confucianism was a religion for the ice age in China; for the revolutionary iconoclasts, Confucianism was the very thing congealed, and anti-Confucianism would melt the ice.

The romantic apologia was not the only recourse of Confucianists. Sometimes they still seemed to plead in a rationalistic spirit, stressing the simple rightness of Confucian doctrine. Thus, we find the familiar kind of statement, vintage 1913 (strained), that the excellent Republic had Confucius as its ancestor. Grouping Confucius with Rousseau and Montesquieu (though, of course, 'their forerunner by some thousands of years'), one Hsüeh Cheng-ch'ing claimed *kung-ho* ('republicanism' in contemporary usage) as Confucius's invention. Yet, Hsüeh's message was really particular, not universal. For the truth of Confucius's idea was not

18

enough. The Chinese Republic notwithstanding—be it validated by ever so many foreign exponents of truth—Hsüeh feared for the existence of the Chinese people if its own teaching, Confucianism, declined.[53]

Again, Confucianism was commended over religions of the outside; as a *jen-tao chiao*, a humanistic creed, it was more advanced than the *shen-tao chiao*, theologies, 'superstitions', of the non-Chinese world.[54] Yet, in the context of Republican iconoclasm, such statements of rational conviction might represent romantic particularism in a special form. It was not the particularism which emphasized that foreign bodies would die if grafted on to the Chinese organism (hence, for example, the hopelessness of the Republic, as it seemed to those who would not enlist Confucius as its advocate). It stressed, rather, that the Chinese organism might die of the intrusion, an intrusion which could indeed take place. Consequently, rational argument, depending on appeals to universal criteria, could rather derive from than challenge a feeling for the national essence, so that a special concern for 'our' religion would drive one to establish it as generally 'better'.

'*Our* religion': Chinese, that is, characteristically and exclusively so, as long as any people could be called Chinese. It was an allegation of permanence, an unshakeable attribute of essence, and safer as an approach to the 'people's will' than any electoral soundings. This was the real trump (and the last card) of Confucianists under the Republic. And whatever their ultimate tactical wish to disengage from Yüan, it was monarchy's card, too. The particular spirit of the Chinese people, not the universal reason of the way of Heaven, became an emperor's justification. 'In today's "people's government",' wrote a monarchist and Confucianist in 1916, 'the model is utterly western. Though in name they perversely call it Chinese (literally, "bend it to China"), in fact, down deep, they know it is not.'[55] Once, republicanism had seemed repulsive to Confucianists as a degradation of human nature.[56] Now, it was a violation of the Chinese nature that repelled an anti-republican.

This new strain of romantic determinism, then, in both

Confucianism and monarchism, ruled out free choice of values; while free choice in the here and now, regardless of historical origins, was the premise for detachment from tradition, the corollary of republican revolution. Nothing could be more constraining than K'ang's lampoon of the anti-Confucian spirit—the equivalent, he bitterly charged, of a desperate will to dye the eyes and make them blue, powder faces and make them white, doctor the hair and make it blond.[57] Chinese traditionalism became a relative, not an absolute principle, a charge upon China, not upon man. Compulsion to preserve the gifts of the Chinese past was psychological now, from an emotional sense of threat to special identity; it was not philosophical, as of old, from an intellectual conviction of the general value of Chinese classic experience. Conservatism and monarchy were welded together, but when novelty was repelled on grounds of the limitations of the Chinese genius rather than on grounds of its fullness or universality, this conservatism was novelty itself. Equally paradoxically this monarchy, trading on the symbols of the past, was itself, no less than the Chinese Republic, a symbol of revolution.

For truly traditional, not merely traditionalistic, Chinese monarchy was ideally monarchy for the world, though centred in one intellectually self-sufficient society. Now, republican nationalistic iconoclasts defined the world as larger than China. They saw Chinese society as very far from intellectually self-sufficient. In reaction monarchist traditionalists, finding it simply impossible in modern times to sustain Chinese cultural pretensions to universality (a Lutheran Norway as justification for a Confucian China!), could preserve the ideal of Chinese monarchy only as monarchy for China alone. And they could preserve the ideal of intellectual self-sufficiency, or renewal of Confucian dominance, only as (something new to Confucianism) 'spirit-of-the-people' imperviousness to new ideas.

Culturally, men who still conceived of Confucian China were much more parochial than their Confucian ancestors, though the latter knew less and cared less about anything non-Chinese.[58] Politically, too, the universal faded. Yüan

Shih-k'ai could not be the 'son of Heaven'; he could only, possibly, be king of China. And Yüan at the winter solstice, miming in the Temple of Heaven (and contemplating ploughing in the spring) was a parody—and not just because he pulled up to the Temple in an armoured car.

Part Two

TENSION AND VITALITY

Almost every party understands how it is in the interest of its own self-preservation that the opposition should not lose all strength.

NIETZSCHE, *The Twilight of the Idols*

CHAPTER II

Confucianism and Monarchy: the Basic Confrontation

YÜAN ends, then, supported by a Confucianism turned inside out. As Confucianism, that is, it still had a commitment to tradition. Yet, the traditionalism, for the most part, no longer derived philosophically from Confucianism. Instead, the Confucianism derived psychologically from traditionalism: when the people's Chinese identity seemed threatened by Republican westernization, the 'Chineseness' of Confucianism, more than its own traditionalist message, made it an object of traditionalists' reverence and a pillar of the throne. Thus, as suggested already, the cement of the 'national spirit' joined the new monarchism and the new Confucianism in a new sort of partnership, new in its rather simple, uncomplicated character in contrast with the devious, uncertain, *tense* partnership of pre-western days. For the classical imperial system, for which Confucianism became philosophy *par excellence*, was founded by Ch'in (221 B.C.) on anti-Confucian Legalist principles, and this paradox, right from the start, remained at the core of Chinese history; a bureaucratic intelligentsia, while it cherished the social stability attending imperial centralization, yet was recurrently centrifugal, hence dangerous to a dynasty, by reason of its acquisitive tendencies. This ancient imperial paradox, which distinguishes true monarchy of the Confucian age from its parody, deserves to be examined.

25

The loss of this ambivalence, this Confucian-monarchical attraction-repulsion, comprised the Chinese state's attrition. And if in its time that traditional state was a very hardy perennial, perhaps its vitality, in a truly Nietzschean sense, was the measure of its tolerance of tensions: their release was the bureaucratic monarchy's death.

1. NOTES OF STRAIN

Over the long span of imperial Chinese history, there developed a Confucian literatus-type; the figure of the emperor failed to conform to it. In many of his cultural and institutional affinities, he offended literati taste. The literati were eclectic enough philosophically, of course, and for any period from 'Warring States' (403–221 B.C.) on, Confucian texts may be shredded into all sorts of ingredients—Taoist, Buddhist, and what-not—but Chinese history does know intellectual confrontations, not just a happy melange, and relatively pure distillations of non-Confucian ideas had tendencies to seem at least in part imperial. Non-philosophical Taoism, for example, jarred on fundamentally rationalistic Confucianists not only in its form of popular 'enthusiasm' but in its connection with the elixir lore often strongly associated with emperors. Buddhism, too, had not only popular backing (often, from late T'ang on, as an anti-gentry, i.e., anti-Confucian, symbol) but imperial patronage as well, in times when its standing was extremely low or at best equivocal among the literati.[1] What could cause more revulsion in Confucianists, with their code of ethical relationships, than the patricidal or fratricidal episodes that disfigured so many imperial family histories? Eunuchs, whom Confucianists scorned and often hated and coupled with monks as 'bad elements', were characteristic members of imperial retinues. Trade, which Confucianists affected to scorn (while Buddhism gave it impetus),[2] was a matter of imperial interest. It was an interest deriving from a court society's demands for luxury, which were not approved by Confucianists, and it was manifest in such various phenomena as the eunuch Cheng Ho's voyages (1403–33), which Confucian historians buried;[3] eunuchs' prominence, protested by officials, in trading-ship control organs;[4] and the Canton system of trade (1759–1839), in which the superintendent, the 'Hoppo', was a specifically imperial appointee and outside the regular bureaucratic chain of command.[5] And the history of aesthetics in China records the distinction, Sung and later, between the 'officials' style' (*shih-ta-fu hua*) and the style of the court academy (*yüan-hua*: see Volume One). The distinction may have been blurred by artistic eclecticism but it was nonetheless significant, for it spoke of the self-detachment of the literati critic, his sensing of a dissonance of gentry and palace tones.[6]

2. THE RELATION TO FEUDALISM

Now, cultural rifts like these were far from extreme, for, after all, the social roles of bureaucracy and monarchy were only clashing, not incompatible, and were complementary even as they clashed. To put it another way: at least from the reign of Han Wu-ti (140–87 B.C.) monarch and civil official had a common stake in anti-feudalism (and in this their interests were complementary), while at the same time each had leanings (and here they clashed) to just that side of feudalism which was poison to the other. The ambivalence of bureaucracy toward monarchy and of monarchy toward bureaucracy was comprehended in the ambivalence of each toward feudalism: bureaucracy had some, at least, of the dynamics of feudalism without the statics, monarchy had the reverse.

The imperial state was the proper milieu for bureaucracy (emperor and official, that is, were to this extent drawn together) in the following sense. A pre-Ch'in nobility, extending back in time from the third century B.C., exploited land withdrawn from the reach of the public power, the would-be imperial state, which thus became a nullity. But the instability which China's political fragmentation portended reduced the private feudal power itself, and in the post-Ch'in empire the feudal nobility was superseded by a bureaucracy, which exploited the power of an anti-feudal state. The centralized state, as the universal tax-gatherer, ideally inhibiting instability, had a basic though ambiguous value to a power-seeking bureaucracy—it provided something rich and real that could be eaten away in the feeding of private power. And it was eaten away recurrently. The process began anew each time the imperial state was reconstituted, after such attrition had brought it toward an impossible (because self-dissolving) feudal dissolution. Bureaucracy, then, perennially suspicious of imperially-backed strong men, with their infinitely various ideas for checking private aggrandizement in land (the *hsien-t'ien*, or 'limit-the-fields', central government policies), was, though abortively, a 'feudalizing' force.

But it was never feudal. Needing the centralized state as it did, after its fashion, the Confucian corps had very serious anti-feudal commitments. As a type, Confucian intellectuality runs counter to the feudal admiration of martial vigour. War is mainly for the young, and Confucian opposition to a chivalric code of heroes was a turn to the elders, to learning over courage, and to a system of examinations of learning as the ideal road to power and prestige, circumventing those juridical guarantees of status which feudalism accorded to birth. And the examinations stressed a *traditional* learning, not original thought, because age over youth means not only counsellor over warrior but old over new—the rule of precedent, the rule of example. Such reverence for precedent may sound close to feudalism, but feudal spokesmen for the most part dwell extensively on tradition only when feudalism is coming to be obsolete and under fire.[7]

However, this Confucian hostility to the 'static' attributes of feudalism implied tension, too, with monarchy. It was a tension explainable socially by monarchy's resistance to that erosion of public power which bureaucracy furthered dynamically, in its own gesture toward feudalism; and it was explainable intellectually by monarchy's leaning to just those feudal attributes that Confucianism countered. For in a feudal system, after all, monarchy has its familiar place at the pinnacle, and, with the marked exception of the feudal propensity for draining the central power (the Confucian bureaucracy's side of feudalism), many feudal associations were Chinese-imperial as well.

Dynasties were not pacifist like Confucianists but military like feudalists, always trying to keep a grip on the Confucian-suspect military organs. To see the divergence, not just of taste but of interest, one has only to watch a Han emperor detouring around his civil bureaucracy, entrusting the military to utter dependants like his relatives in the female line.[8] The Confucian ideal, embodied in the examination system and model-emperor lore, of non-inheritance of political standing, was inapplicable to hereditary monarchy, as it was to a feudal system in the round. It is probably in this connection that the Confucian sage-emperor lore had some of its greatest significance. The pre-Hsia period of Yao and Shun (the sagest of the sage) was sometimes referred to as the 'Yao Shun *shan-jang* era'; and the *shan-jang* convention for solemnizing an imperial abdication and succession was a convention for transmission of the throne to one of a different surname.[9] What was the *shan-jang* idea (projected into the past by Confucianists) but an expression of Confucian anti-dynastic feeling? It was after Yao and Shun, who chose their successors by the Confucian criterion of virtue, not the feudal criterion of hereditary right, that dynasties began: a falling off.

And monarchs were vaguely compromised in Confucian eyes not only by their quasi-feudal aura but by the simulated feudal systems which dynasties successively created and literati continually condemned. 'Nothing did more harm to the people,' wrote Ch'ing historians of the Ming period, 'than the *huang-chuang* and *chuang-t'ien* (villas) of the princes and princesses, eunuchs and nobles.'[10] We should note the emphasis on eunuchs and aristocrats, both non-bureaucratic types, and both having corporate existence only as imperial appendages.

It may be assumed that in the full light of imperial history, after classical antiquity, enfeoffment did not represent any genuine monarchical sentiment for feudal fragmentation of the state. Rather, the monarch allowed the existence of what was after all a shadow feudal structure—never with a weight of power to threaten the bureaucracy's—because the state was bureaucratically centralized enough to survive it. And the monarchy willed the existence of this feudal structure because bureaucratic centralization had its inner seed of dissolution. The imperially patronized nominal feudal system —in most dynasties mainly an extended imperial family affair—was of such a character as to be safe for the emperor as long as gentry-literati-officials were with him, while it symbolized his awareness of their potential defection. There is something more to this; I shall recur to it.

From the monarchy's side, too, the priority of family might be deplored. The Confucian *hsiao*, filial piety, was potentially irreconcilable with *chung*, political loyalty, an imperial requirement as well as originally a feudal conception;[11] while on their side Confucianists (especially of the Sung variety), at least in their ideals, tended to moralize *chung* as they had moralized other originally feudal concepts. They accepted loyalty as an obligation, but they meant to impose their definition of loyalty upon the emperor, not to have simply a blind requirement imposed upon themselves. As the neo-Confucianist Ch'eng Hao (1032–85) put it, the emperor must distinguish between those who are loyal and those who are disloyal.[12] This imperative implies a Confucian sense of discrimination. The onus is on the emperor. Loyalty may not be defined as unquestioning obedience to his (perhaps improper) wishes. Rather the advice or example (the same thing) of a true Confucianist demonstrates loyalty, and the emperor should recognize that those who agree with such sage advice are the loyal ones.

3. THE RELATION TO LAW

And when it came to the rule of law (more acceptable in feudal than in Confucian society), Ch'in Shih Huang-ti (246–210 B.C.) was the Legalist and truly the First Emperor, the prototype. For the codes were imperial and their very existence was an implied rebuke to emperors, whose virtue, thought Confucianists, was evidently not enough to make for a flawless (law-less) social order.[13] A Stoic parallel in the

Greek and Roman world (the Stoics, like the Confucianists, stressed harmony rather than action) corroborates the logic of this anti-legalist deprecation of actual monarchical power. Like the Confucianists again, the Stoics were far from admitting the unqualified legitimacy of contemporary absolute monarchy. Only the Sage, they felt, is capable of absolute royal rule, and he rules by calling others to imitation of himself (Cicero, *De Legibus* and *De Republica*). Possessing reason in himself, he can dispense with written laws; he is the living law.[14]

Just so, in the *Analects* (*Lun-yü* VI, 29) Confucius refuses to credit a ruler with *jen* (human-heartedness) if he makes a 'wide conferring on the people' and shows 'ability to aid the multitudes'. Exerting the inner force of sage example: only this, to Confucius, is the technique of *jen*. But in actual history many monarchs had social programmes, or at least made protestations, of 'wide conferring on the people', and many Confucianists deplored them. In ultimate Confucian terms these would be *yung* without *t'i*, action without essence, programmes of compulsion (merely Legalist) without the essential Confucian *jen* to compel them to exist.

This all sounds very high-minded, to be sure, and a sceptic may see only a cover for material interest, gentry resentment of monarchical land-tenure schemes or the like. But this opinion, while too cynically reductive, simply reflects the fact that the Confucianist as a social person and the Confucian intellectual come together; he demonstrates in both these aspects his distance from the monarch (yet also his place in the monarchical system, a solar system of gravitational ties). When the Sung scholar Ch'en Liang (1143–94) professed to discern sage-king patterns not merely in classical high antiquity but in the prosaically historical Han and T'ang dynasties, Chu Hsi (1130–1200), incomparably more in-fluential, denounced him, and with appropriate emphasis stressed *hsiu-chi*, self-cultivation—the 'inner' pole of a famous Confucian dichotomy—over the 'outer' pole, *chih-jen*, ruling men.[15] Morality, the inner test which non-ideal, actual monarchs do not pass, transcends the legally constituted externals.

4. THE FACTOR OF FOREIGN CONQUESTS

The over-all distinction between the necessary partners, Confucian literati and monarchy, and the basic condition of the tension between them, lay in their respective attitudes toward tradition. Here Ch'in Shih Huang-ti again, at the beginning, and the *T'ien-wang* of the Taipings (1850–64) near the end, seem the purest representatives of anti-literati, anti-traditional, undiluted monarchy. They were too pure to survive, too unequivocally unrestricted, without that blurring of the timeless monarchical abstraction which could make them historically viable; dynasties in general had to make the adjustments these disdained with traditionalist Confucianism.

But the adjustments came from practical necessity, not from the genius of the institution of Chinese monarchy itself. One who contemplates the relation of monarchy to bureaucracy from this standpoint may reverse a familiar emphasis: perhaps the real issue is not the degree to which alien dynasties proved acceptable to Chinese literati, but the degree to which native dynasties proved alien to them. In the complex of Chinese political society, foreign dynasties may well have been nothing peculiar, only native dynasties to a higher power, and ethnic distinction no special problem of bureaucratic-dynastic relations, only an exacerbation of the endemic problem of the division of powers. A foreign conquest-people and its chiefs might well in their hearts be culturally out of touch with the ideals of the literati. But so, to some extent, would be any Chinese Court.

What Manchu prerogatives represented to Ch'ing Confucianists, the prerogatives of eunuchs may have represented to their predecessors under the Ming. And eunuchs or no, Manchus or no—as long as monarchs kept a sense of proportion, and never faced the literati with too rich an alien mixture—Ming and Ch'ing were dynasties that Confucianists could live with. The Taipings' anti-Manchu propaganda was symbolic, perhaps, of a nationalistic revulsion from gentry culture, an ethnic displacement of a cultural Chinese identity. But it was a sham as an anti-Ch'ing weapon. For the gentry-literati-Confucianists were ostensibly more likely than any other Chinese to respond to an anti-Manchu call, since they suffered from the unfair proportion of Manchus to Chinese in high governing circles, while nineteenth-century peasants could barely have known Manchus as such. Yet, the Confucianists were loyal. They felt no special ethnic revulsion from the Manchus, but simply an expected strain between monarchical and bureaucratic bodies, a strain far less traumatic than the Taiping break.

Indeed, as the almost immediate dissolution of the Manchu people in twentieth-century Republican China would show, the Manchus were kept afloat by the Ch'ing dynasty, not the dynasty by the Manchus. Thus, ultimately, their foreignness must have been barely more than the permissible (though censurable) foreignness of monarchy itself. The Yüan dynasty (1279-1368), in this respect, had not been like the Ch'ing: as that Mongol dynasty rebuffed and repelled the Chinese literati more than the Manchus were to do, so it preserved its internal integrity with far greater persistence. The Mongols as a people did not vanish with Yüan.

Of course Confucianists were susceptible to anti-foreignism. As we have seen in Volume One, Confucianism held centrally to the amateur ideal, countering specialization, the vocational training of men who were to be merely used as instruments. Confucianists opposed depersonalization, and that is why they emphasized the humanities even in (or especially in) their education for office: they were to be ends, not means, not a monarch's tools. Indeed, for Confucianists, one of the qualities that tainted the monarch's province of law was its air of impersonality and abstraction. (Wherever, it seems, 'experts' are disliked and the amateur ideal encouraged, the instruments of legal transaction tend to be technically weak.)[16]

Now, hostility to foreigners, particularly ethnic minorities, tends to focus on stereotypes, and impersonality and special role are the very stuff of stereotypes. Ethnic assimilation implies the break-up of the 'specialized' image, as the group disperses into the whole variety of human possibilities. In China, in so far as conquest dynasties forbade assimilation, they limited their cohorts in social scope and clapped them into specialized roles. Indisputably their foreignness made for tense relations with Confucian literati; but it was a Chinese ethnic antipathy reducible to Confucian cultural terms. When, as the special tools of their foreign-dynastic leaders, they aroused ethnocentric feeling among the literati, this was not just gross discrimination, native against foreign. They were really offending a finer sensibility—anti-specialist and anti-despotic.

While the Ch'ing's Manchus had their military examinations, the Chinese scholars who sneered at 'the scholarship of a Manchu' were expressing distaste for the specialized garrison type, or stereotype. Impersonal, dehumanized by association with a special function—so the Manchu might appear in Chinese eyes. But it was a cultural appearance and a political one; race was not the crime. Race only made it plausible that a Manchu should seem to be wholly owned and operated. That was the crime. And it was not a mortal one for the Manchus, since Confucianists needed monarchs, and monarchs, native or foreign, had such a penchant for control.

By this token, the familiar statement that pre-nationalistic culturalism legitimized any patrons of Confucianism, whatever their ethnic background, can be stated more precisely as follows: Any dynastic establishment, whatever its ethnic background, had the same need to patronize (failing at its peril) but *also the same need to qualify* Confucianism. It was not that foreign dynasties should meet some minimum of expected cultural conformity; it was rather that foreign dynasties should practise no more non-conformity than a maximum expected of rulers in general and grudgingly allowed them. It is because this was the state of affairs that we find Confucianism, for its part, always needing monarchy and always assuming its existence, but always implying restraints on its innate waywardness.

CHAPTER III

The Evolution of the Confucian Bureaucratic Personality

I. ARISTOCRACY, MONARCHY, BUREAUCRACY: TRIO IN THREE MOVEMENTS

THE 'Doctrine of the Mean' is one of the 'Four Books', familiar to Confucian-trained officials from the Southern Sung period to the end of Ch'ing, from the thirteenth century to the twentieth. The metaphysical aim for dead centre, 'the still point of the turning world', where harmony had its Confucian apotheosis, was politically true. Since the officials' culture favoured the study of history, they were well acquainted with the Chou period of local aristocracies and the subsequent Ch'in period, that famous burst of the utterly despotic. And it was the genius of Confucian bureaucracy (though not always its achievement) to be poised between the poles of local and central power, magnetized to both, and resisting in its values the final claims of either. If one speaks one-sidedly of Confucian (bureaucratic)–monarchical tension as the major motif in imperial Chinese history, this is because aristocracy in the technical sense, with its perquisites and hereditary status, though never dying, generally languished. But the aristocratic ideal, as a rival for Confucianism to banish—in part by resistance and in part by pre-emption—fixed the bureaucracy's location as surely as the royal reality on the other side of the centre.

Consider the perennial question of alienability of land. At least sporadically, both Chou nobility and later monarchs

C.C.—D 35

tried to impair it, the former in a spirit of feudal inequality, the latter in pursuit of an anti-feudal despotic egalitarianism.[1] By and large the bureaucracy, public officials with private interests, set itself against this expression of both an ultimate resistance to the public power and its ultimate pretension. In the main, bureaucracy defended the right to alienate (and its corollary, to accumulate by purchase), a right that was just as opposed to a power-inhibiting feudalism's premise, as it was to the most extreme of a power-seeking monarch's desiderata. And on the same intermediate line, Confucianists favoured undivided large-family holdings—social expression of the 'harmony' which Confucianists as philosophers so incessantly commended. This was equidistant from feudal primogeniture, on the one hand, and the centralizers' policy (against the threat of local concentrations) of pressing for fragmentation by exacting dues progressively according to the number of a household's adult males.[2]

When cultural rather than economic values come under review, Confucianist and aristocrat clash just as vividly. Both agree that there is something about a soldier, but not on what it is. The Confucianist, after all, is the eternal civilian. In *The Romance of the Three Kingdoms*, after Ts'ao Ts'ao has some of his stalwarts do wonderful martial feats, he summons a few tame scholars whom he keeps around, 'stuffed with learning', to produce *their* tricks. They snap to attention on the spot with some canned Confucian poesy in praise of their warlike patron. Here, in a form of literature which Confucianists on duty never approved of, in a setting of the decay of the Han, the first of the bureaucratic, centralizing dynasties which 'established' Confucianism, this flash of contempt for the Confucian higher life exposes it appropriately against the counter-value of military prowess.[3]

In feudal Chou China, men were thought of in four categories, in descending order of esteem: *shih, nung, kung, shang*—warrior, farmer, artisan, merchant. By the middle of the first millennium, B.C., with feudalism crumbling, the warrior-class of *shih* was losing power and inferiors were rising.[4] When supremacy finally passed to a bureaucracy of the Confucian persuasion, the four categories were still retained (an example of what Confucianists meant by their 'perpetuation of feudal values', while really they created anew), but *shih*, designating precisely the power group, changed its connotation, from military to literary.

It was characteristically Confucian on the one hand to retain the old term, as a traditional piety, and on the other hand to 'moralize' it (as Confucius did to *chün*, prince, or as Mencius to the *kung* of *kung-t'ien*, which had the sense of 'noble's' field in the *Shih-ching*, the 'Book of Songs', but 'public' field in Mencius' picture of the 'well-field' system). To moralize it was to 'civilize' it, quite literally. *Wen-hua*, the Confucianists' 'civilization', was plainly an enshrinement of *the civil; wen*, letters, and *wu*, arms, always remained in antithesis. Right at the end of Confucian history, in the early twentieth century, a Chinese nationalist and former Confucianist, Liang Ch'i-ch'ao (1873–1929), admired the evolution (as he saw it) in Japan of self-transcending feudal loyalties to national loyalties, and deplored the Confucian extinction of *shih* as devotees of *wu*, the capture of the title, *shih*, by pacific literati. He said that *wu-shih tao*, the 'way of the warrior' (in Japanese the *bushidō* of modern chauvinists and mediaeval aristocrats), had flourished up to the 'Spring and Autumn' period, dwindled to knight-errantry by the beginning of Han (the beginning of Confucian ascendancy), and soon was nothing.[5]

In fact, however, aristocracy as a serious contender with Confucian bureaucracy in its own right—not just as an imperial auxiliary—seems not to have been silenced conclusively until the Sung period (960–1279). The Sung, in this way, too, as in others, was one of the great watersheds in Chinese history. With Sung, both the institutions of bureaucracy and the formulations of Confucianism were highly elaborated, and they were such as to spell effective triumph for *wen* over *wu*. Previously T'ang (618–906) had seen the link forged, with the examination system, between intellectual life and bureaucratic power, and heard the last cry of the *men-t'i*, 'social notables', as they felt themselves cordoned off. Li Te-yü (787–849), for example, hated the *chin-shih*, high degree-holders, the new men rising through the bureaucratic channel. He said defiantly that since his grandfather's time as minister (at the end of the reign of Hsüan-tsung, mid-eighth century, just before the An Lu-shan rebellion), the family had not acquired literature and classics, for these had no relation to skills and practicality. The great officials of the court, he said, ought to be drawn from the *kung-ch'ing*, the aristocratic lineages.[6]

In such a statement, aristocracy's discomfiture is plain to see. The menace of Confucian bureaucracy seems confirmed by the pitch of aristocratic resentment. But more than that, it is the aristocrat's 'bureaucratized' self-image that marks so clearly the lowering of his estate. He offers himself as a superior brand of official, knowing practical statecraft—a monarch's man, that is, no longer someone with the typically fierce aristocratic resistance to an autocrat's infringement on nobility's prerogatives. Indeed, the crown had so nearly triumphed over the classical pretensions of aristocracy that the pattern of three has rearranged itself.

Aristocracy had been an impediment, in Chou times, during most of the first millennium, B.C., to centralized authority. And though aristocracy was blighted by the autocratic Ch'in, it was seriously revived from the third century A.D., in the post-Han period of hollow dynasties and military conquests. Stricken by T'ang, it moved to the side of *monarchy*. *Bureaucracy*, the Ch'in–Han and later the T'ang instrument of anti-feudal monarchy, now confronted the crown directly; after helping to clear the field of the crown's rivals, it held the field itself as the only remaining countervailing force. The monarch, served to such good effect by bureaucracy that aristocracy was tamed, repelled bureaucracy in some degree by his now unbalanced power. And Confucianists, who owed their corporate existence to imperial sponsorship in the teeth of aristocracy's hostility, took up the role of resistance when the aristocrats' teeth were blunted. Aristocrats, now the monarch's creatures, sounded more and more like kept men, while Confucian officials strained to get out of the monarchy's keeping. And so while some aristocrats became Confucian enough to see themselves in a bureaucratic context, but approached a monarch's non-Confucian ideal of a bureaucracy of means, Confucianists took on some aristo-cratic colour, conceived of themselves as ends in themselves, and set out to prise open the imperial clutch.

There are a series of steps in the minuet thus described. I should like to examine them one by one.

2. BUREAUCRACY AS THE MONARCH'S TOOL TO CHECK ARISTOCRACY

It is a commonplace that feudal aristocratic status was based on private possession of essentially public powers, private exercise of public executive functions. The anti-feudal 'public' is the state (a community, as Weber defined it, that successfully claims monopoly of the legitimate use of force within a territory), or the public is the prince who makes the state by expropriating the 'autonomous' and 'private' bearers of executive power.[7] As Montesquieu put it flatly, 'abolish the privileges of the lords, the clergy and cities in a monarchy, and you will soon have a popular state, or else a despotic government'.[8]

Conservative apologists for aristocratic institutions have always made much of this connection between autocracy and a 'public's' obliteration of rank and its privileges. What makes despotism characteristically arbitrary is the despot's ability to raise and lower his subjects at will. The infinite power of such a sovereign depends on basic equality beneath the throne, so that no guaranteed distinctions exist between men to spoil the infinite malleability of the body politic.[9] Orwell speaks of 'an idea almost as old as history', the idea of King and the common people in a sort of alliance against the upper classes.[10] In the Peasants' Revolt in Germany (1525), for example, the readiness to attribute real authority to the Holy Roman Emperor was identical with the passion for destroying aristocracy.[11]

World history yields many plain illustrations of this model issue between sovereign and aristocracy. In the later Roman Empire in the West, the aristocratic Senate saw in such a bureaucratizing emperor as Valentinian I (364–75) only a proletarian's hatred for his betters. For while members of the senatorial party, as incipient feudalists, were building estates by sheltering fugitives from the tax rolls and sequestering their lands, the emperor tried to preserve his central power by bureaucratically undercutting this protection racket of the great lords. The new imperial institution of *defensor plebis* was meant to guarantee the poor peasant a free legal defence. Naturally, with such a policy, Valentinian pushed senators well into the background when he staffed his bureaucracy; he could pit only special aides against the senatorial oligarchy, cohorts who leaned on him alone, because he made them.[12]

If effective monarchy was one that bureaucratically encroached on aristocracy, enfeebled monarchy spoke for the centralizers' failure to impinge on private powers. Thus, reflecting Valentinian's ill success and the fading of the Roman imperium, the imperial post of 'vicar of the city' (fourth–sixth century) failed to remain a counterpoise to the senatorial 'prefect of the city'. And as the supremacy of the great senatorial landholders became more and more unmistakable, subverting the imperial social order, the central government tried to survive by binding subjects to their home places and inherited lots in life—by freezing social mobility.[13] This was the cure that guaranteed demise. This, the exertion of a spurious despotic power, was the sacrifice of the purest power of unharassed autocracy: the power to co-opt whom it pleases and raze the defences of class.

Such was the power claimed naturally by a monarch with truly oecumenical pretensions. The 'lawbook of Melfi' of the dazzling Hohenstaufen Frederick II (1194–1250) has been styled 'the birth certificate of modern bureaucracy'. Flashing briefly to the heights of rulership he drew men to his service not with the *beneficium*, a fief to possess, but with the *officium*, a service to fulfil. Non-transferable and non-hereditary, office was his alone to give, his to repossess, graced with his grace. He made officers from any rank, and no considerations of rank could mitigate the power of his omnipresent hand—his bureaucracy.[14]

Byzantium, which filtered Roman imperial conceptions through to Frederick, did the same for Russian czars. In the sixteenth century Ivan IV ('The Terrible') flouted old

Kievan aristocratic ideas and sapped the position of the noble boyars with a band of faithful servants, the Oprichnina, chosen without regard to class, for Ivan called all his subjects 'slaves'. The boyars recovered sufficiently by the next century to stand off, weakly, the new régime of the Romanovs— social privileges retained, but political power unreplenished.[15] And here we have a suggestion of the 'Sun King's' arrangement in contemporary France, a tactic fateful for the future of French monarchy and provocative to the observer of Chinese.

What Louis XIV did after the various rebellious actions of the Fronde (the nobles' and the *parlements*', 1648–53) was to bring new men to power, but to separate actual power from apparent grandeur. He meant to preserve a politically shorn but socially splendid aristocracy so that its political supplanter, the king's bureaucracy, should be cut off from the social dignity which could make it aristocratic itself, and thus a potential rival, not a tool. The very model of an autocrat speaks in Louis' words: '. . . it was not in my interest to seek men of more eminent station because . . . it was important that the public should know, from the rank of those whom I chose to serve me, that I had no intention of sharing my power with them. (It was also important) that they themselves, conscious of what they were, should conceive no higher aspirations than those which I chose to permit.'[16] Louis' 'intendants', their very title a new creation, took over the government of the countryside from a nobility either soothingly sinecured (the 'sleeping abbots', et al.) or ineffectually rustic or emptily grand at Versailles, where the king and his bourgeois ministers left only something of war and something of diplomacy to the heirs of feudal greatness.[17] Before Richelieu, the centralizing genius behind Louis' achievement, the king demanded fidelity; after (an important nuance) he exacted submission.[18] The Duc de Saint-Simon complained that Louis surrounded himself with nothing but 'vile bourgeois'. Saint-Simon, of course, was in favour of an aristocratic reaction against royal absolutism (and especially against the bureaucratic secretaries of state, whom he described as monsters devouring the *noblesse*). But reluctantly he ascribed the failure of the Regent's aristocratically weighted 'Polysynodie', in the first years after Louis XIV, to the emptiness of a nobility good for nothing but getting itself killed in war.[19] That was the Richelieu effect: the monarchy absolute, nobility dissolute, and its autonomous powers dissolved.[20]

This refers primarily to the *noblesse d'épee*, the old 'nobility of the sword'. The newer *noblesse de robe* was still to be heard from, leading the movement in the eighteenth century for aristocratic revival, and I shall take note of this soon. But the initial attempt (though it proved abortive) to make the king omnipotent remains highly suggestive. The conception of an aristocracy still in being, but sterile and ornamental, has a part in a logic of absolutism. And the logic applies in other lands as well.

In Prussia the French emphases were altered but the triumvirate was there; monarchy, bureaucracy, and aristocracy still confronted each other. Frederick William I, in the first half of the eighteenth century, looked for ministers, he said, who were ordinary persons (or, indeed, 'yapping little dogs'), less intent on their honour than aristocrats, who might refuse him blind obedience. The Hohenzollerns eventually softened their approach and compromised between a Junker aristocratic 'private law state' (a spoils system of patronage appointment) and a dynastic bureaucratized 'public law state' (merit appointment of experts). Still, though the monarch never pushed the bureaucratic attack on the nobles to a logical culmination, the hereditary noble 'officier' and the upstart royal 'commissaire' were distinguishable types, which had their distinctive relations with the monarch. The government of Frederick William I, like that of Louis XIV, had an unmistakably bourgeois impulse in it, and this accorded with the basic character of the *ancien régime*. It was a character formed by the accommodation of aristocracy to absolute monarchy, an accommodation whereby aristocratic social privilege was preserved, while the nobility was politically transformed. These civil relations of aristocracy and monarch reflected a power-shift in military relations—from the feudal nobility's abhorrence of the emerging monarch's 'public' armed forces, to the monarch's re-furbishing of the status-honour of nobles, in their new *personae* as the members of his officer corps. As they were *his*, they were damaged in their aristocratic licence; but as they were *officers*, they were still aristocratic.[21]

What those aristocratic-bureaucratic-monarchical rela-tions involved (as surely in China as in the western examples) was tension between a centralizing power and vested interests. Some of the latter were feudal-aristocratic, impeding a monarchy's rise or expediting its fall; and some were bureau-cratic, new, and of the monarch's own contriving as he asserted himself against the aristocracy. Resolutions differed from place to place, but everywhere the tension was an auto-crat's concern. When Ch'in united the Chinese Empire against the feudal hierarchies, which were territorially and jurisdictionally divisive, and when it determined to stave off re-feudalization, it had an appropriate motto, an anti-hierarchical one: 'When fathers and elder brothers possess the Empire, younger sons and brothers are low common men.'[22] Han emperors acted decisively on a Confucianist's advice to dilute the ranks of nobles of the Liu (the imperial) family, and drain their strength; it was a strength which had served the Han against nobles 'of different surnames', but which central authority had to fear when the rivals common to all the Lius were duly vanquished.[23] An early T'ang hereditary aristocracy, flourishing in its natural environment of military conquest, was deliberately subverted by Empress Wu (684–705), who conjured up a royal, rival class of literati from an 'open' examination system.[24] And a thousand years later the Ch'ing Emperor Yung-cheng (1722–35) showed the same penchant of autocrats for levelling up, this time from the bottom: he ordered that various local pariah peoples—the Shansi *lo-hu*, descendants of families with a criminal stigma; Chekiang *to-min*, 'fallen people', and *chiu-hsing yü-hu*, the endogamous 'fishing people of the nine surnames'; Anhui *shih-p'u*, 'slaves'—be officially treated without distinction from others of better standing.[25] This is a standard type of anti-feudal measure, part of a programme to flatten status barriers against effective central power (like Meiji dismissal of the legal disabilities of Japanese pariahs, the *tokushu buraku*, 'special villages' of *eta*).

Yung-cheng, however, and the Ch'ing dynasty were on the far side of the great divide, the Sung. In that earlier period, though 'outside lords' were already effectively extinguished and the weight was shifting definitively toward bureaucracy and autocracy, the emperor could still seem poised (and sometimes paralysed) between his aristocratic near relations and his bureaucratic aides.[26] But by early Ch'ing there could be no question of the emperor in the middle. He was at one of the poles, and though Yung-cheng had an aristocracy around him, he owned it. Confucian bureaucracy, the guarantor of the harmlessness of nobles, had long since been the status group whose solidarity autocrats had to melt. And formal aristocracy, gratifyingly choked off by bureaucracy as a major threat to the monarch, was fanned into life as part of the flame to be turned against its stifler.

3. ARISTOCRACY AS THE MONARCH'S TOOL TO CHECK BUREAUCRACY

The founder of the Ming dynasty in 1368, an autocratic centralizer with the best of them, nevertheless, with his eyes wide open, provided for enfeoffment of imperial princes. He hardly intended to let it get out of hand, and regular bureaucrats were to supervise the princes' troops and communications. Then, presumably safely subject to the centre and incapable of disintegrative mischief, they were supposed to be converted to the centre's support. The main threat in the early Ming was Mongol. But what the monarch cared about was defence against infringement of the imperial power in any case, by invader or official. Enfeoffment, hopefully *controlled*, so that by itself it should breed no rivals to the throne, was a dynastic response to eccentric forces from any rival quarter.[27]

The Ch'ing, too, had an aristocracy of their own as an anchor against the bureaucratic drift. The Manchu conquest meant that villas of the Ming imperial family nobility and much other land lay abandoned, without owners. Part of it was taken over by the Ch'ing imperial house, part was given to deserving officials and the like who had come with the winners from Manchuria. In 1650 the dynasty established a regular system of land allotment to various grades of feudal notables, from *ch'in-wang*, hereditary princes (8 *so*, every *so* being 180 *mou* or about 27 acres) down to *feng-en chiang-chün* (60 *mou*). This scale applied to subsequent ennoblements. The lands were all hereditary and *inalienable*.[28]

This feudal conception, so much at odds with the predominant social practice, was clearly meant to invest the imperial house with an aristocratic bulwark, shored up against the solvent forces of the general Confucian society. Yet, to render the aristocrats themselves harmless, the dynasty used a Confucian technique, an examination system, and controlled them bureaucratically. The rules called for tests in archery and the Manchu language, to be administered four times annually by the 'Court of the Imperial Clan' to not yet enfeoffed or not yet adult sons of nobles; and in the examination in the first month of winter, overseen by a specially appointed imperial high official, not only sons but the lesser nobles, too (with fiefs ranging down from 240 *mou*) were subject to the trial.[29]

How effective, really, could these Ming and Ch'ing aristocracies be as checks on the regular officialdom? They were so hedged in themselves that they were hardly impressive as restraints in the world outside. Rather than putting a positive curb on Confucian bureaucracy, they represented, perhaps, the monarch's attempt to withdraw, for associates of his own, some stores of strength from the field open to official depredations. To cut down actively on the latter and thus preserve his power, the monarch needed private bureaucratic agents more than aristocratic consumers. These agents should form a personal corps, depending on him for honour and place, therefore approaching the despotic ideal in bureaucracy: a set of instruments. This was just the ideal which Confucianists resisted—once the eclipse of aristocracy had made them and *their* honour less dependent on the throne.

Therefore, in the last analysis not 'princes' and 'dukes' but eunuchs and simple Manchus became the centralizer's tools. Indeed, even a millennium and a half before the Manchu era,

Han emperors were feeling pushed to marshal a 'third force', in this instance eunuchs, to weigh against the Confucian element, and the scholars were duly recording disapproval.[30] They disapproved less of the T'ang practice of appointing eunuchs to check on the deviationism of military commanders[31]—the latter were no great favourites either in Confucian circles. Still, the lesson was the same: eunuchs, despised by literati, were used by the emperor personally to guard his central power. However (to make the comparison more immediate), at the Ch'ing courts, even the relatively indulgent Empress Dowager's, eunuchs were markedly fewer and more strictly restrained than under the Ming.[32] This suggests again what we have already suggested, that eunuchs and Manchus, in the Sino-foreign, Ming and Ch'ing dynastic sequence, were functionally equivalent. For by themselves Manchus would play the role of auxiliaries well enough, outsiders thrown back on the monarch who made them— made them both in spite and because of the literati's resentment.

And what was the nature of this resentment? Of all things, it had a certain aristocratic air about it, as befitted a self-regarding group's contempt for mere dependants, the men from nowhere who needed a monarch to guarantee their rise. If this sounds like a Han or T'ang aristocratic resentment of the Confucianists themselves, it is no accident. When the older, vital aristocrats went down as the Chinese imperial power became transcendent, the Confucianists' self-regard became the monarch's concern—for would they be loyal to him?—and the Confucianists' self-regard withered the newer recruits to the monarch's loyal coterie.

4. THE CONFUCIAN BUREAUCRACY'S RESISTANCE

That the literati felt lofty enough to scorn this sort of coterie confirms the fact that a monarch needed to own such objects of scorn. That is, aristocracy was no longer lofty enough itself in social prestige to monopolize it, and so divorce it (like Versailles from Louis XIV's intendants) from the officials' political functions. The officials, accordingly, were not so bound to the crown. Failing any serious competition from a rival elite (feudal aristocracy being so curtailed), feeling no social gaucherie in comparison, Confucian officials could have an aristocratic pride of their own, unvitiated by the self-doubts of the *arriviste*—theirs was the circle where climbers yearned to arrive. They themselves, functionaries though they were, set the tone of culture instead of facing the scorn of the functionless, like the late Bourbon politically stripped aristocrats, who dismissed local government as the province of clowns and clerks.[33] Chinese emperors could neither deprive bureaucracy initially of that formidable combination, prestige and executive function, nor dangle before it subsequently, as prizes (and seeds of obligation), titles conveying lustre from a truly noble estate, beyond bureaucracy.

Prussian kings eventually did the latter. Since the Junkers had by no means utterly succumbed to Frederick William I's 'yapping little dogs', the 'von' was still precious enough for the *nouveaux* to covet—while the king was both autocratic enough to give it, and not quite autocratic enough to banish the need or obliterate the glory of the gift. Bureaucratic 'nobles of ascent' began to meet feudal 'nobles of descent', with the latter now constrained to join the bureaucratic endeavour, and ultimately even to mingle with commoners on the basis of *Bildung*, a new cultural bond. *Bildung*, an amorphous but deep feeling for an inner moral and intellectual cultivation, impaired the monarch's ability to impose himself as master and impose on officials the character of tools. Old nobility, to some extent cut down to bureaucratic stature, preserved and spread some aristocratic resistance to the centre; and new bureaucratic nobility, for all its dynastic and anti-aristocratic origins, became set in reaction against royal autocracy and competition in government service. As a Königsberg colleague of Kant remarked in 1799: 'The Prussian state, far from being an unlimited monarchy, is but a thinly veiled aristocracy—this aristocracy rules the country in undisguised form as a bureaucracy.'[34]

Confucianists came to their resistance by a different road. In Prussia there was some degree of devolution of aristocracy to bureaucracy. But the hybrid form at the end of the (pre-

Napoleonic) process—an intellectualized conception of aristocracy—was remarkably like the Chinese amalgam. Seeing the process as evolution towards rather than devolution from aristocracy, we may read the hybrid the other (and even more clumsy) way round, 'aristocratized intellectualism', but the Prussian analogy is surely compelling. The future statesman Wilhelm von Humboldt, writing in 1789 and after about how 'one forms oneself' ('man *bildet* sich'), prized freedom and anti-despotic self-mastery, general culture over useful knowledge. He felt contempt for the philistine who lived to work and worked toward material goals, and he stood for things and states of mind valuable in themselves, for men who were more than things, for ends over means.[35] A Confucian '*Bildung*', infused with the same spirit of anti-vocational, humanistic amateur ideal, had the same implications of tension with autocracy.

What *Bildung* meant, and what Confucian cultivation meant, was the achievement and vindication of a kind of prestige which was not the monarch's to confer. In an unmitigated despotism, the government employee is the most vulnerable of men, totally insecure in his legal status and social standing.[36] But a Confucian official, non-vocationally educated, was no mere 'employee'. He might be summarily retired, even executed, or he might retire in self-abnegation, but his dignity and social status were not destroyed; for regular official position was taken as a sign of a quality (high culture, not simply professional expertise) which existed irrespective of the holding of office. The Confucianist brought it to office, not office (as the monarch's gift) to him. And if a monarch lacks the sole power to confer prestige, he cannot enslave his bureaucracy by threatening to withhold it.

Thus, the submergence of true aristocracy gave Confucian bureaucracy something of the latter's quality. But while officials strained against the monarchy, they needed it, as the guarantor of a central power that had to exist for them to enjoy consuming it. It was an ambiguous position, reflected, perhaps, in the ambiguous status of Mandarin, the *Kuan-hua* or modern 'officials' language' (being the standard speech of the capital, effectively Peking from fairly early Ming to mid-Republic). During imperial days Mandarin was by no means secure in its prestige, since with the more rapid phonetic changes in the north it had lost ancient distinctions which central and southern dialects had preserved. There were grounds for fastidious—one might say aristocratic—reserve towards this linguistic instrument of the centralizing power.[37] Yet, scholarly sophisticates were, after all, bound up in the bureaucratic system, and Mandarin, from being useful as the officials' *lingua franca*, went on to assume an aristocratic tone of its own. It was not exactly a language of the happy few—not with millions of commoners tuned in on its sounds—but it took on the distinction of guild speech (and a proud guild, surely), transcending the provincial associations of common local dialect.

So, in and out of the monarch's service, drawn to it and drawing back, Confucianists might seem to speak out of both sides of their mouths. And the monarch was just as ambiguous. For he needed them to make good his centralization; then, in turn, to protect it, he had to restrain their ominous appetites. Therefore, even in flouting Confucian taste, the emperor might pander to it in his covering explanation. For example, after the Yung-lo emperor usurped the throne in 1403, he had his historians libel his ousted nephew as a patron of Buddhists and eunuchs. As it happened, the really active recruiter of monks and eunuchs had been Yung-lo himself,[38] with the autocrat's feel for the usefulness of a personal force of outsiders, as a check on the orthodox element that he needed to win and needed to keep. Thus, Yung-lo could not just counter Confucianists nakedly with Buddhists and eunuchs; he had to indulge these anti-Confucian coteries, then mask it with a Confucianist's apology.

This was the monarch's side of the line of strain. He might resent the hierarchical tone of Confucianism as he resented aristocracy's, but if he failed to indulge Confucianists in their quasi-aristocratic taste for freedom and status, he risked the ultimate Ch'in fate of bureaucratic and general revulsion. On their side, Confucianists had to acknowledge that if they strained against the centre too successfully, they might deliver themselves as well as the state to a host of brutal

49

Ts'ao Ts'aos. That is why monarchy could be despotically Legalist, military, and yet the patron of Confucianists; why bureaucracy could be aristocratically Confucian, pacifist, and yet the agent of monarchs; why, inclusively, Confucianism persisted not only in tension with monarchy, but in tension within itself.

CHAPTER IV

Confucianism and Confucianism: the Basic Confrontation

I. INNER AND OUTER

BENJAMIN SCHWARTZ has pointed out an ambivalence in Confucian thinking, a persistent wavering between concern for the 'inner' and concern for the 'outer', though a symbiosis of both concerns was in theory essential. The spheres of *nei* and *wai*, that is, inner and outer, were considered interrelated, so that (in a famous phrase) *hsiu-shen* (or *hsiu-chi*) and *p'ing t'ien-hsia* were joined ideally in one concept. Self-cultivation and world-pacification must imply each other; if there is a true *sage* (sageliness being a quality of inner perfection), he should properly make an outside mark on the world, as the true king.[1] And yet, Confucianists as historians have known that imperfect 'kings' (or men with the unrectified name of 'king') have done most of the ruling, while at least one of the sages, Confucius himself, was notoriously a 'throneless' king. The great founding historian Ssu-ma Ch'ien (145–90? B.C.) made the classical contrast between powerless but memorable Confucius and powerful but forgotten (or ultimately uninfluential) monarchs.[2]

This gives Confucian historical thinking much of its pathos. Knowledge and action (another inner-outer dichotomy) should be one, but the 'times', the mysterious 'times', so often thrust them apart. 'Though Confucius had *te*, virtue, he did not attain *i*, position':[3] those who know, in the Confucian sense, cannot act. Or they *should* not act, as Confucian officials, under monarchs who are in the supreme position to act, but who do not *know*. The note is there in a neo-Confucian poet: 'When one is born in a degenerate and disorderly age, and there is no one worthy of being called a ruler, who would want to serve? . . .[4]

Han Yü (768–824), the first great figure of 'neo-Confucianism', had adumbrated this idea. The T'ang scholar drew on Mencius' authority to urge Confucian independence of a court's demands, and Confucian scorn of the merely time-serving, court-manipulated, unprincipled official.[5] This leaning to the 'inner' pole became a characteristic of neo-Confucianism—witness the strictures on monarchy which Chu Hsi implied when he firmly separated the age of sage-kings from the ages that came after[6]—but the inner-outer ambivalence was never banished. On such a question as the reinstitution of the *ching-t'ien* (well-field) system, there was conflict among Confucianists and indeed in individual minds (see Volume Three). For they had a social, outer commitment to strive for perfect governance, a commitment which coincided with the monarchical interest in curbing private aggrandizement in land; and they had an inner commitment to morality, as against the force that would be needed to wrest the land, in egalitarian spirit, from acquisitive possessors like the bureaucrats themselves.

2. PRIVATE AND PUBLIC

To say (like Chu Hsi) that *ching-t'ien* could not be revived was as much as to say that the outer world, the province of kingly government, was too badly flawed to accept perfect institutions without having them forced on it. And to that side of Confucianism leaning to inner morality, the outer application of force (proof that an emperor was falling short of a sage's emanation of virtue) must compromise the value of the effort. But to the side of Confucianism leaning to ethical obligation out in society, such quietist defeatism was uncongenial. So it was to Wang An-shih (1021–86), for example;

though certainly Confucian, he was the very type of centralizing, imperial strong man, and action, necessarily imperial, was recommended. To the defenders (mostly officials or the officially well-connected) of the material interests threatened by such action—precisely the 'private' interests which the 'public' state intended to curtail—the moral reproach to the central power was invaluable. For all the fact that when Han Yü excoriated court sycophants he was condemning the pursuit of advantage instead of morality, advantage could quote morality for its purposes. Unimpeachable moral heroes like Han Yü provided a treasury of grace, a store of the highest-minded anti-despotic feeling, for self-indulgent materialists to raid. Perhaps that is why, like some other idiosyncratic individuals, of really questionable orthodoxy, he could finally go down in Confucian history as so uncannily orthodox.

Thus, the lines are drawn, but they are very blurred and wavy, with Confucianism on both sides, just as bureaucracy was on both sides of the issue of central power. Chu Hsi praised the famous reformer Fan Chung-yen (989–1052), but praised him for his moral character (the basic subject in Confucian critiques of emperors), not especially for his reformist action (which was of a sort that monarchs always found in their interest, for its strengthening of the central apparatus).[7]

3. FAMILY AND CLAN

Fan Chung-yen was prominent in another capacity, one that also fits into the framework of the bureaucracy-monarchy problem. The system of clan properties and formal organization in China, which Fan was so important in moulding, is at issue here. There was an imperial influence on clan rules, appropriately in the Legalist strain;[8] the state had a plausible interest in furthering clan organization, since aid to the clan implied transcendence of the family. It was an interest in a certain kind of collectivity, which might preclude a system of family atoms, ranged in classes, and therefore likely to collapse into the wrong kind of social combinations.

Monarchy, with its ultimately levelling propensities (as seen in the centralizers' perennial ideal of land-equalization) sought to enlist the clan idea of vertical solidarity, i.e. class *un*consciousness, as a check against social fissure on a horizontal line.

And yet, if the clan became the family writ large, any high degree of social autonomy for clans might seem an assault on the state toward the ends of private power, and so the clan itself became subject to imperial restriction.[9] The family was supposed to have its proto-feudal possibilities diluted in the classless clan; but the clan should have its own strength, which it collected from its family components, re-divided so that the state might safely rule. In effect, the post-Sung state moved ambivalently to break down potential private power, by checking the clan with family and family with clan. And Confucian sentiments could be marshalled for both these operations.

When clan leaders, impelled by clan loyalties, acted to soften state pressures against their more obscure fellows, the clan, even while it thus resisted the central authority on an *ad hoc* basis, was serving it generally by diffusing the benefit of gentry status throughout the social system. This suited the monarch's anti-aristocratic purposes, his will to keep officials and their affiliates from hardening into a quasi-aristocracy. And in this he had the officials and clan leaders at least as much with him as against him. For one of the alternatives to clan solidarity was a freemasonry of the secret societies, which cut across clan lines in uniting lower-class dissidents against the state; neither Confucian leaders, with their zeal for harmony, nor monarchs, whatever their straining against each other, could countenance this.[10] Indeed, in as much as secret societies implied potential rebellion, and rebellion implied a decisive (hence upsetting) commitment to a cause, ambivalent wills were just what the party of order, in counterpart, should naturally display. For ambivalence, fundamental as it was to Chinese monarchy and bureaucracy, within each one and toward the other (if not toward popular, unambivalent class-violence), is nothing if not the forswearing of decisive single-mindedness.

4. CHARACTER AND SCHOLARSHIP

One of the important functions of the clan organization was to spread more widely the opportunities for education, and thus for socially valuable success in the state examinations. The monarchist central power would naturally be interested in this at two historical removes—first, approvingly, because the examination idea was incompatible with counter-imperial feudal assumptions; and second, warily, because once the examination was well established the monarch had to guard against the development of a potentially divisive, hardened power-class perpetuating itself by simple capture of the examination system. In 962, out of fear of cliques, the founder of the Sung dynasty forbade use of the terms *tso-chu* ('master') and *men-sheng* ('disciple') between successful candidates and examination administrators.[11] The Ch'ing's thoroughly and self-consciously authoritarian Yung-cheng emperor felt particularly queasy about this. In his zeal against factions he wanted no undue solidarity among officials, and he was endlessly suspicious of ties and cover-ups—the fellow-feeling of examinees of the same year, of examinees and their examiners, other such bonds and alignments.[12] Responding nicely to such suspicion, and corroborating its rationale, was an eighteenth-century careerist, calculatingly slavish, wilfully seeking friendlessness (or so it was said) to commend himself directly to the emperor.[13]

For its part, the Confucian bureaucracy, too, held the examination system both dear and suspect. In many ways it expressed what was most characteristic in the Confucianists' existence, and one of the ways was in its challenge to non-literati, precisely imperial types like eunuchs and soldiers. The latter, for instance, in the Ch'ing dynasty, were frequently able as new men to penetrate bureaucracy and to compete with literati in seniority—doing violence to Confucian pride by rising in wartime, *sans* classical study and literary tests.[14] Thus, the civil Confucianists had to keep on insisting that these tests gave a special cachet.

But if the system were operated with a cold, impersonal purity, with no room for 'character' (often, in practice, equated with lineage) to come to the fore, the Confucian sense of hierarchy might thereby be flouted by a levelling monarch. There were early Ming examination laws directed against the older official families, as the emperor, meaning to thwart this taste for hierarchy, tried to hold the ring for new plebeian contestants.[15] What the emperor tried to contain was just the sort of sentiment, a discriminating feeling for status, which tinged Confucianism with aristocratic colour. In the T'ang period, when the examination system was formalized as the Confucian channel of mobility, aristocrats (like Li Te-yü, as we have seen) had protested in defence of 'character'. Men of good family favoured direct recommendation; new men needed impartial examinations.[16] The examination question, an issue between aristocrats and Confucianists in T'ang times, when these groupings still contended, was intra-Confucian thereafter.

David Nivison, dwelling on the examination system, caught the ambivalence of the Confucian position (and, one might think, its not unrelated vitality) in his splendidly circular title, 'Protest against Conventions and Conventions of Protest'.[17] The protest was fundamentally one against the conquest of spontaneity by rote. Now, why should spontaneity be a Confucian value? This problem was treated in Volume One, with its discussion of Chinese literati-painting (significantly opposed, we have seen, to 'court painters' and the imperial 'academy'), and, with something of Mr. Nivison's sense of being driven to paradox, I committed myself to the mouthful, 'academic anti-academicism'.[18] If the intellectual derivation of literati-painting's aesthetic was neo-Confucian,[19] this seems the philosophical corollary of my own rather sociological thesis of the painting-Confucianism affinity—a thesis stressing the *anti-professional* bias of the bureaucrat. As a professional the official would be simply a functionary, an imperial tool. But as an amateur, the official would be a free spirit, not the organizational mandarin whom the centralizing authorities so dearly loved to cultivate, and 'spontaneity' was the Confucian key to this precious non-attachment.

If Greek education was designed to produce gentlemen

amateurs, while 'eastern' education (i.e., Egyptian) was designed to perpetuate a guild of professional scribes,[20] the Confucianists were Greek. And yet they were 'eastern', too, at least a little—ambivalent—for, unlike the Greek paidaeia, Confucian education led to bureaucracy in the end. And yet, again (back over the net): it was not an 'Egyptian' scribal bureaucracy, but a system in which the bureaucrats could dominate society, or at least tense the line between themselves and intrusive monarchs.

The imperial academy of painting, it has been observed, was created in the Northern Sung period for substantially the same purposes and with many of the same characteristics as the Académie Française that glorified Louis XIV.[21] The analogy with Louis points to the monarch's will to make tools of his subordinates; the Confucian critique of the academy points to the Chinese literati's resistance. And the resistance was far from token, since the anti-academic aesthetic became 'official', in both senses of the word: the bureaucracy set the styles, not the monarchy, for the values of the Chinese world.

And yet the anti-academic became academicized, the protests against convention became conventional, because, after all, the very examination system which enshrined a liberal, anti-vocational learning stressing high culture and moral character made that learning *useful* though not utilitarian. Thus, inevitably, men *did* direct their study to an end which was not itself and became subject to condemnation from their own standpoint, as rote-trained, unspontaneous, manipulable placemen, not self-cultivated with an inner independence—*little* men in an imperial apparatus. Small wonder, then, that there was scope for a truly Confucian fear lest moral character be slighted in a quasi-Legalist impersonal machinery of stereotyped tests. For all the fact that the examination system was a distinguishing mark of Confucian civilization, a *sine qua non* for Confucianists' social prominence, it was still a Confucian morality that expressed itself in various modes of circumventing the state examinations.

Original Confucian requirements (anti-feudal in the sense of raising 'character' and 'culture' above lineage and military command) had led, then to an examination system which seemed to violate Confucian requirements in so far as it raised culture above character in the would-be official's concerns. After all, learning was, but morality was not, susceptible of systematic testing. Since the system could be seen as splitting what Confucianism saw ideally as inseparable, good character and high culture, the anti-examination Confucianist, not admitting the possibility of the split, condemned, as stereotyped, the 'culture' fostered by the test. 'Some said, "The learning of the examinations corrupts men's minds. Recently the scholars read only poems and essays to plagiarize and do not take any notice of how important it is to cultivate one's moral standard and govern oneself." '[22]

One of the tentative detours around the examination system, supposed to have some relevance to 'character', was *yin* privilege, whereby the official distinction of fathers gave easier bureaucratic entree to sons. Here a hereditary factor, quasi-aristocratic but with the 'family' note Confucian, after all, impinged somewhat on the anti-feudal Confucian idea of careers open to talent. *Yin* privilege was particularly associated with conquest dynasties.[23] We suggested, in analysing the basic confrontation of Confucianism and monarchy, that native dynasty and conquest dynasty were both aliens in the world of the Confucian ideal. Differences were in degree but not in kind. We may now put it another way: if the domestic was just as alien as the foreign (or a little less so) in its tension with Confucianism, the foreign was just as native as the domestic (or a little more so) in setting up Confucianism for tension within itself.

5. PRECEDENT AND RULES

The Confucian-Legalist (literati-imperial) ambiguity of the examination system was just a version of the ambiguity of 'precedent', which in different lights was a Confucian or Legalist value. True authority (if one may speak tautologically) is ultimately bound by nothing, including precedent. The despotic Ch'in Shih Huang-ti, burning the books and burying the scholars, knew it well. Hence, Confucianists strained against Legalist monarchy in their capacity as traditionalists—like the aristocratic Senators, straining against Valentinian in defence of the traditions of Rome.[24] But the establishment of *rule* (i.e., precedent in the Legalist sense) is the key to an unspontaneous controlled bureaucracy; it was the monarch and his centralizers who stressed *fa*, law, method, rule. Precedent, then, so richly entitled to Confucianists' respect, could be subversive of Confucianism, and to the Confucianists the examination system, with its similar potential, was both suspect and indispensable.

6. FREEDOM AND SURVEILLANCE

And so it was to the monarch. In so far as he and his Confucianists (not his, too) were both on all sides of the examination issue, so he and they, in general bureaucratic dispositions, seemed to give and take with one hand what they took and gave with the other. In the Ch'ing period, for example, we see the emperor forced to choose between two of an autocrat's objectives, political safety and administrative efficiency. One man would be appointed to several offices, several offices to one function (which was rarely defined precisely).[25] This certainly, and gratifyingly for the monarch, made it difficult for officials to dig themselves in. But it could not add up to a 'modern' bureaucracy, the rationalized corps of experts which a central power ideally would command. It rather conformed to the literati ideal of amateur omnicompetence. Yet, it was in his own interest that the monarch made his bureaucracy thus. What was that interest, but to check the bureaucracy's pull against him? And how was the pull exerted, if not by the very character-type, that of the amateur-independent, which his rulings contrived to restrain so well, yet also contrived to harden?

CHAPTER V

Confucianism and Monarchy: the Limits of Despotic Control

I. MORALISM

IF the examination culture tended to stereotype and staleness, Confucianists developed both a commitment to the routine and misgivings about it. The imperial attitude was ambivalent, too. The monarch was a centralizer who might deplore stereotypes, as obstructing his officials' effectiveness. But as a centralizer he was also seeking his officials' docility, and to that end he was well served by the pressure of stereotype against 'inner' spontaneity, the sign of an 'inner' moralism which could serve as a restraint on him.

We have already met the theme of Confucian moral strictures against force, which was a prerogative that monarchs naturally assumed for themselves, and morality indeed was the Confucian approach to monarchical restraint. The nature of dynastic succession (as distinct from bureaucratic appointment) being what it is, royal legitimacy in China could not possibly be subject to any formal examination of cultural attainment, and the morality which had to be left out of the bureaucrats' tests had to be left in the Confucian assessment of monarchs. The early stereotype of the dynasty's 'bad last emperor' showed how the very Confucian respect for the monarch, as holder of the *T'ien-ming* or 'mandate of Heaven', and thus first in a moral hierarchy, furnished the grounds for censure[1]—and for Confucian preservation, since the moral fire on dynasties protectively screened the officials' material system.

We have observed that a genuinely Confucian concern about satisfying the *min*, the people, carried no implications of 'democracy', Caesarist or otherwise. On the contrary, it was essentially Confucian to reject majority rule, with all its air of impersonal, mathematical abstraction. But if the strongest in numbers were not to rule, the strongest in power would, and brute power was no more congenial to Confucianists than impersonal number. Still, individuals, unlike faceless masses, have moral possibilities, so Confucianists had attached themselves to emperors. While a dynasty worked, they covered its monarchs with a veneer of morality; this would gloss over (to their emotional and the monarch's political advantage) the actual basis of rule, sheer power. When Confucianists hypocritically, even slavishly, ascribed morality to an emperor, they seemed indeed his creatures. But this very morality, or the assumption that he required it and that they could judge it, was the mark of their independence—co-dependence, to put it a little lower.

2. LOYALTY

Yet, we face the problem of the shift away from 'bad last emperor' judgments in later Chinese history. Certainly from Sung, there was strong Confucian insistence on loyalty to an emperor one had served, a loyalty which committed an old official not to serve a new dynasty.[2] This seems hard to reconcile with the 'mandate' response, moralistic revulsion from a last emperor, and recognition of the line which effectively succeeded. Should we conclude that the emperor now was truly irreproachable, and officials at last were really only tools? But Confucianists never completely yielded to monarchs what the latter always sought, the right to define *chung*, 'loyalty'. A whole sea of Confucian feeling against the simple equation of loyalty with obedience was distilled in an episode of the *Tung Chou lieh-kuo chih*, in its last revisions a late Ming novel. A minister kills himself—as an expression of the higher loyalty *to his ruler*—when he fails to persuade the latter, with the following proposition, that he should spare the life of a friend: 'When the ruler is right and the friend is wrong, one should oppose his friend and obey the ruler; when the friend is right and the ruler is wrong, he should disobey the ruler and follow the friend.'[3]

Confucian disapproval of the transfer of loyalty from a deposed dynasty to its successor was a way of refurbishing, not destroying, the official's self-image as end, not means—not vocationally educated, hence not professional, hence not bound. The *ch'en-chün* relationship, minister to monarch, was one of the *personal* relationships so prominent in Confucianism, and a minister's loyalty, then, was no sign that an imperial owner disposed of him completely, but rather a sign that the minister *was* a person, not a thing—not a cog in a bureaucratic wheel that kept on turning, whatever the Legalist dynasty that generated the power. Confucian refusal to serve (unlike Taoist withdrawal) was an affirmation that public service was a high ideal, so high that it must not be compromised by dishonourable conditions. Honour counted, more than the deprived sovereign's (and the deceased sovereign's) pressure.

Chao Meng-fu, the famous painter, calligrapher, and relative of Sung emperors, became an official under the Yüan. Confucianists, who condemned him for disloyalty, were certainly not acknowledging a despotic right (the Yüan emperors') to command him into service. The seventeenth-century Ch'ing *i-lao*, 'Ming remnants', who refused to serve the Ch'ing—and were not dragooned or markedly harassed—were not chained to a dead emperor; they were keeping free of a living one. The authority was classical (Book of History, Analects, Mencius): the example of Po I, who starved himself to death rather than shift his loyalty from Shang to Chou. It was a counsel of moral freedom, not surrender.

3. TERROR

Especially in the Ming period (and especially near the beginning and the end), we find officials being assisted to death in great numbers and in terrifying ways. This was sometimes accompanied by self-abasement, the subject's protestation, even in his last anguish, of his loyalty to the ruler-torturer: '. . . my body belongs to my ruler-father. . . .'[4] Was this surrender, the achievement of absolute despotism, the snapping of tension with the snapping of Confucianists' fibre?

It is hard to say whether this is social or psychological evidence. Observations under desperate modern conditions, in the concentration camps of Europe, have disclosed the possibility of morbid attachments between victims and tor-menters. Still, even if the spectacle of submissive contrition, not defiance, is given a thoroughly social significance, it is not a conclusive sign of uncontested power. For one thing, 'ruler-father' was more than a pitiful lapse into childishness under pressure of the extreme exertion of unrestrained authority. It is generally agreed that monarchical absolutism did increase from Sung through Ming, but this filial language existed quite apart from that development. It was already there in T'ang, perhaps expressing the new elite's affinity with monarchs, during the crucial stage of the conflict with aristocracy: 'In that time (eighth century) ministers called their *chün-fu*, their ruler-father, "sage".'[5]

But more important: a father and son have a *personal* con-nection. It is a *relationship*—implying, it is true, subordination (even the material body may be offered up). But tools have no human relationship, they are used; things are not sub-ordinate, they are owned; while the Confucian official *in extremis*, whatever his inner quality or his practical helpless-ness, still speaks in the language of humanistic culture. Though his sovereign disown him and abuse him, he will not in his total person be a thing or a tool; he will acknowledge a father, yet not an owner-despot. He has no price, and when he serves and dies he has not been bought and squandered. He has value. Though the monarch put an end to his life, he cannot end the Confucian self-image of the princely man (though lower than his prince) as an end in himself.

4. THE PIE OF POWER

Still, fine words pickle no bean-cakes. Officials were often humiliated at the Ming court, to say the least of it, and there were other unmistakable signs that Sung had bequeathed its successors an enhanced imperial power. But there is more to the Ming imperial situation than meets the eye. If Ming was an age of heightened despotism, a monarchical prerogative, it was also an age of heightened traditionalism, the special care of the culturally conservative Confucianists. And traditionalism, we noted, is not the prescription for un-trammelled imperial power. Traditionalism, rather, is one kind of intellectual demand which despotism, in the pursuit of its absolute, always needs to check.

There seems, then, to be a confrontation here, even an incompatibility. But there is nothing incompatible about the enhancement of monarchy and the enhancement of Confucian bureaucracy at the same time. We need not think in terms of just one set of mutually exclusive alternatives, as though one should sum up the later dynastic world in the emperor as the One in the state, the bureaucrats as nothing. Such an assump-tion is not entirely misleading, for it indicates quite rightly that in the end, before the western intrusion, bureaucracy and monarchy were the only real contestants—not aristo-cracy, long since worn away, and not capitalists, who never got away. Aristocrats dropped back in Sung, merchants came forward, but in bureaucratic reins. These are groups which certainly did lack power. But if we ask who took it from them, who inhibited their growth, we find bureaucracy the inhibitor, quite as much as monarchy. Learning and captur-ing hauteur from aristocrats, Confucian officials sustained it against merchants, and in Sung and Ming, at any rate, they grew as much as the monarchs in self-esteem and substance.

In short, with Sung, monarch and bureaucracy got wider slices of the pie of power, until other consumers were pushed from the table, to feed on crumbs. Undoubtedly, the crown had fed its despotism. Yet, even though officials felt the weight of it, they were buoyed up by added weight of their own. Sung centralizers (and after them Yüan, Ming and early Ch'ing) made the capital city the true centre of politics; they reduced the regional powers, especially the military. After Northern Sung itself, no other dynasty was founded by the *chieh-tu-shih* type, the restless independent regional warlord. This was good for the imperial interest, and it left its mark on officials, whose individual standing was rendered more precarious. But it was good for their interest, too, to see a check on the armed usurpers of their own civilian influence. If the individual official was lowered in his standing, yet he rose with his estate.

That is why Northern Sung Confucianists, writing with a seemingly Legalist concern for enriching and strengthening the state, were not so inconsistent. They were not necessarily puppets, doing all for the imperial master and nothing for the old Confucian tradition of the minister's integrity. For now, when Confucian bureaucracy (like monarchy) had increased its power within the state, a more powerful state meant a goodlier portion for the whole man.

5. THE 'SUPREME ULTIMATE'

Along these lines, another paradox can be riddled out. Certain Sung Confucianists, especially the great historian Ssu-ma Kuang (1019–86), undeniably magnified the emperor more than earlier Confucianists had. Yet, he was one of the opponents of Wang An-shih, that centralizing activist with strong imperial support. Our question is not why Wang had enemies (the reasons are many and complex), but how the hostility fitted in with the will to exalt the emperor. Perhaps the answer is this. First, when Confucianists came into their own it was with, not against, the raising of the monarch: they both enjoyed reducing the same rivals. But second, 'coming into their own' implied awareness of a need to defend themselves, to resist Wang, to resist anything that might appear as an autocratic raid on their position. They owed the prize to the autocrat, and repaid him with awe. But just because they prized it they cherished it against all comers, including the prize-giver.

If on its political side neo-Confucianism was far from slavishly imperial, metaphysically, too, it was by no means categorically pro-despotic. What connection may we establish between *t'ai-chi*, Sung philosophy's 'supreme ultimate', and the supreme ruler in the Sung political conception? *T'ai-chi* is the norm of norms, the form of forms; it is immanent, impersonal, and passive, having logical priority but nothing of the creative priority, the active power, of transcendental monarchy. As we shall see, when the nineteenth-century Taipings assailed Confucianism and raised up a monarchy of truly transcendent, absolute pretensions, their 'supreme ultimate' (*Shang-ti*, not *t'ai-chi*) was neither impersonal, passive, nor immanent, but their own version of the Lord of Hosts. On the level of casual mental association, to be sure, the Sung hierarchy of concepts—with room for just one at the top—might carry over to reinforce a hierarchy of men. Yet, psychology aside, if there is any systematic relation between *t'ai-chi* and the scope of imperial power, that relation is to the quietist strain in Confucian political thought, the immanentist, anti-power emphasis on the Son of Heaven's necessary virtue.

Perhaps, then, imperial confirmation of the neo-Confucian *li-hsüeh*, this Sung rationalism, as orthodox and mandatory has sometimes been over-interpreted. It need not be taken to prove that monarchs at last had a perfect Confucian rationalization for their purposes, nor that the Confucian establishment had finally become a wholly-owned subsidiary. The imperially sanctioned neo-Confucian monopoly came about not because, in itself, the philosophy flattered the monarch, but because in itself (i.e., in intellectual terms, not political) it was impressive enough to be an orthodoxy: it was intellectually possible to name and accept it as such. We ought not to be super-political here, implying that it was imperial fiat alone that made it orthodox. It is enough that monarchy appreciated the *li-hsüeh*, as a politically useful gift from intellectually powerful thinkers—useful, because intellectual orthodoxy would foster intellectual docility, with political docility as a by-product. Useful, too, because the monarch's seal on the orthodox learning would give the scholars a *quid pro quo*, subsidy in return for loyal support. And if the scholar had support to offer, some power to sell for his *quid*, the monarch still fell somewhere short of monopoly. There was more than One in the state.

66

In sum: the development of despotism at the centre, in early modern Chinese history (from Sung into Ch'ing), did not preclude (nor should its description overshadow) the development of a stronger position for bureaucratic Confucianists. They had a feast of agreement with monarchs on the spoils of aristocracy. And, just as much as monarchs, or rather more, they skimmed off or squeezed from the increasing product of mercantile activity, and grew with the companies. They were not abject; they were still in a position to strain against the power that might make them so. The picture of Ming imperial horrors perpetrated against hapless officials and gentry needs a balancing picture, perhaps one of the 'Wu culture' of confident gentleman-amateurs,[6] at a humanistic summit of refinement, unshrivelled by terror—and just as quintessentially 'Ming'.

6. UNIVERSAL DOMINION

Just as the seemingly absolute dynastic claim on loyalty may well have been ambiguous, so even the famous ceremony of prostration before the emperor, the *k'ou-t'ou* (kow-tow) cannot be viewed simply as 'the great symbol of total submission' of the Confucian bureaucracy.[7] The gesture dramatized a *Confucian* conception of imperial power, a conception that went so far beyond Legalist monarchy's own requirements that it hints, paradoxically, at a submission far from total. This act of abject deference identified a monarch infinitely high because his mandate of Heaven, his *T'ien-ming*, made him Vicar of Heaven on earth. The earth was all that was *T'ien-hsia*, all 'under-Heaven'—and Confucianists at an early date used this formulation in support of their own authority, when Buddhism threatened its political basis, challenged its universality. Originally, eloquent Chinese monks claimed to be in the world but not of it. For Confucianists, anyone who was in the world was in the Empire (*T'ien-hsia*, too), hence subject to (the officials of) the holder of *T'ien-ming*.[8]

Now, it is not for nothing that scholars sometimes render

fa-chia, the 'Legalist' party of the Ch'in founders of the imperial dynastic system, as 'Realists'. As the winners and holders of power by force (the 'virtue' gloss was Confucian, something ideologically useful to emperors, and suspect: another inner tension), dynasts were ready, being practical men, to define their world not as *the* world, but as the area where their writ could possibly run. This might impel them to conquest, out to Tibet or Turkestan or the like. But at least such regions were militarily accessible. Beyond that, monarchs could leave the merely metaphysical power claims to Confucian spokesmen.

Perhaps that is why, after Chinese envoys to Moscow in 1731 performed the kowtow before the Russian Czarina, the record of this interesting act was preserved only in a Russian source, and not in any Chinese.[9] Did Confucian recorders suppress it because such a gesture to a sovereign outside their system clashed with their idea (not necessarily their monarch's) of universal kingship? Why should the redoubtable Yung-cheng emperor, whose claims to absolute power in China were not modest, seem to give more licence to envoys in a matter touching his dignity than Confucian archivists were willing to give? Was it because a Confucianist could not, and a Chinese monarch could, sanction a Chinese kowtow in Russia which would make uncertain the *Confucian* implication of a Russian kowtow (or any other) in China? This Confucian implication included, first, in its identification of the Confucianists' monarch with the world's monarch, recognition of the universal supreme value of Chinese culture (a characteristically Confucian, not a monarchical tenet). And it included, second, in the very 'mandate' conception which justified monopoly of power and the appropriate gesture of abasement, a reminder of the monarch's moral responsibility. The allegiance of 'tributary states' to Chinese emperors enhanced the imperial prestige—but in a cautionary Confucian manner. For such acceptance of Chinese suzerainty, for the very reason that it often went unenforced by military strength, could be understood as a dramatization of 'dominion through virtue', which Confucianism conferred on no dynastic line as an inalienable right.

68

Yung-cheng might exact the kowtow in China and appreciate it there, as a flattering recognition of the power he exerted where, realistically, he could expect to exert it. But when he sent a mission abroad he was free, consistent with his own understanding of power, to step out of the character, the universal role, ascribed to him by Confucianists, whose conception of kowtow made it not only flattering but potentially inhibiting. Doubtless, on his own home ground, Yung-cheng was pleased to receive kowtow as a symbol of total submission. But the ceremony suited not only dynastic but bureaucratic preferences, for Confucianists attached a rider to the monarch's interpretation, endowed him philosophically (not materially) with an authority over far more than home ground, and in their very hyper-inflation of his power proclaimed their own integrity, as its judges. Nietzsche suggests that to serve, not curb, their will to power, men may impose their own chains[10]—or their own kowtow?

7. FACTION

Yung-cheng knew well enough that no symbolic procedure like kowtow assured him of perfect peace with a docile bureaucracy. He acknowledged this by bringing the relationship's contradiction into the open. We have already seen that he meant to guard the examination system from what he construed as factional abuse. What he feared was possible combination, the banding of quasi-aristocrats against his authority, and he singled out a famous Sung official for posthumous chastisement. 'Yü-cheng p'eng-tang lun' ('Imperially corrected "on cliques and factions" '), 1724, was his answer to Ou-yang Hsiu's essay of 1004, which had argued a case for beneficial factions: even filial obligation, said the emperor, must give way to the demands of office.[11] He was not nominating himself as 'ruler-father', metaphor that was still within the Confucian realm of discourse. He was not building a bridge of connotation, but disconnecting, with painful literalness, a Confucian filial obligation from an imperial demand.

Yung-cheng's ideal was an autocracy in which officials

fanned out from a single point of concentration, the emperor, with no individual connections between official and official. There were to be no groupings which would make so bold as to voice a literati 'public opinion'. When an edict was handed down, he proclaimed in 1726, his only consideration was its conformity to reason, to the needs of the situation, not in the slightest to any group's preferences. As part of his argument against bureaucratic faction, he dismissed 'public opinion' as a matter of 'small men trying to cover up their own deficiencies by making warped judgments on the empire'. And in all this he made the supremely autocratic assumption that he was acting on the basis of a famous principle of the *Lun-yü*, the 'Confucian Analects' (VIII, ix): 'The Master said, "The people may be made to follow a path of action, but they may not be made to understand it." '[12] One could hardly be more insulting to officialdom. For it was one thing when the Confucianists, hierarchically minded, spoke of the *min*, 'the people', in this fashion; it was another thing, a levelling act of monarchy, when the emperor implied that officials were *min* themselves.

It is no wonder, then, that Yung-cheng earned the reputation of relying more on law than on moral influence. His fetish was efficiency, a ruler's word and an engineer's word; in neither association, in one no more than the other, did it chime sweetly with the Confucian tone. As with the tone, so with the tactics. Yung-cheng got some efficiency (probably more than any other Manchu ruler) largely because of his checks against corruption, his vigilant surveillance.[13]

Yung-cheng tried to impress local officials with his burdens. In a touchingly confiding edict he told them of a tablet at the entrance to his chambers, with three characters on it, *wei chün nan*, 'It is hard to be the ruler.' On two sides of a pillar there were hanging scrolls with antithetical messages, 'It is the responsibility of one man to govern the empire', and 'It is not the responsibility of the empire to serve one man.'[14] The sentiment seems Confucian, but, for all the self-immolating devotion to duty, emphasis is on the one man. He knew his supreme and solitary place.

8. VIRTUE, POWER, AND IMPOTENCE

And yet he knew, too, what a strain it was to get there, a strain against Confucian bureaucracy. Even he, even his grandly self-assertive son, the Ch'ien-lung emperor (1736–96), with the balance of power tipped sharply toward the throne and away from bureaucracy, still spoke Confucian political language. Ch'ien-lung scoffed at the idea of a sovereign dwelling 'in lofty seclusion, cultivating his virtue'.[15] He had the power to scoff; but still, he had to exert that power against a moralistic conception of monarchy.

Maybe he, too, found restraint something he needed for his own good. The officials had it in kowtow, self-aggrandizement through self-abasement, as they quietly reserved, the harder they knocked, their Confucian right to judge. Just so, when the monarch acknowledged their right, with its implied impairment of the fullness of his power, he fulfilled a vital condition for holding the ample power he retained. The fetters of a master: was his burden of virtue a chain that *he* imposed, as well as his colleague-rivals? For a monarch whose virtue is unassailable may be unrestrainable. But also, he may be nothing more than a symbol, always Good King George while his ministers make the record—maybe blameworthy folly, but *they* make it.

In China, the very insistence by Confucianists, however muted, that imperial virtue had something to do with what happened in history, and could be impugned by it, kept the emperor inside the arena of power (while it gave the arena walls). He was not elevated to impotence, to that empyrean height where only officials had real responsibility—in both senses, executive and moral.

9. THE STATE AND THE IMPERIAL HOUSE

Thus, Ch'ien-lung clung to power. He did it, paradoxically, by accepting a world in which Confucian censure was always latently possible. And he did it, in further paradox, by grandly refusing to entertain any hint of Confucian censure. Representing power, precisely what Confucianists were striving to restrain, he made in all consistency an imperial variation on a characteristic Confucian judgment. As we have seen, those literati who opposed the revival of *ching-t'ien* (the stylized classical 'well-field' system of co-operative land-tenure, with its air of public-spiritedness) gave up on that institution—perfect though they acknowledged it—because the virtue of emperors had fallen off after the sage-kings' era. And therefore, these critics felt, only the force of inadmissible power could bring the *ching-t'ien* back, not the solely permissible, yet impossible force of morality.[16] Ch'ien-lung, however, complacently gave other grounds for his own scepticism about *ching-t'ien*: it was the nature of modern *man* (no mention of monarchs, and certainly no suggestion of self-indictment) which had grown meaner—'Who is willing to put public ahead of private interest?'[17]

And who was willing to call his own interest private, while others presumably protected the public? Yung-cheng took pains to impute private, anti-state interests to officials: 'The phrase *ta-kung wu-ssu*, public, not private, sums up what We expect of officials.'[18] It was a clear case of state versus estates, as the centralizing monarch, in the universal pattern of counter-feudalism, identified his own conquest of power with the emergence of the public interest. But although Chinese dynasties ended feudalism, they did not create the modern state—which is only to say that Confucian bureaucracy was never the professional bureaucracy of experts which joined the European princes on their modern rise to power. The Confucianists remained independent enough and became aristocratic enough to call the monarch's encroachment not public but private itself. It was the prince, charged the most extreme of the Confucian critics (like the seventeenth-century scholar, Huang Tsung-hsi), who treated the empire as *his* estate, who made *ssu* where there should be *kung*.[19] Huang's contemporary, T'ang Chen, put it most bitterly: 'From the Ch'in, monarchs have been bandits. The prince became aggrandized, the people became his sheep and pigs.'[20]

However one interpreted the fusing of the 'public' interest with the private imperial interest—whether as the emperor's plunder or the state's restraint on private plunderers—

certain dynasties, the Ch'ing among them, made the ultimate claim that, technically, all land was imperial land. The standing principle of the Ch'ing dynasty was, 'Court and government are one essence.' But this was merely a verbal formulation; it did no more than formally ascribe full power to the imperial house. Actually, as the early nineteenth-century *Chia-ching hui-tien* indicates, a distinction between government land and imperial land was preserved. The categories of *t'un-t'ien* (military fields), *mu-t'i* (pastoral land), *hsüeh-t'ien* (study fields), etc., were government. Imperial property, the monarchical interest as 'private', had its own designation, *chuang-t'ien* (villas).[21] Just as land in the Ch'ing period generally was alienable, hence not really the emperor's or 'nationalized' (depending on one's interpretation of the intrusive role of the monarch), so this distinction between government and imperial lands shows the reality of private property. Neither monarchs nor Confucianists could convincingly maintain that their opposite numbers imposed the selfishness of *ssu* on the Chinese world, or establish that they themselves stood unequivocally for *kung*.

This was the tension between companions, Chinese monarch and Chinese bureaucracy, which only the Taiping Rebellion (1850–64) finally began to resolve. Until that beginning of the post-traditional era, the monarchy, standing for central power, worked against the bureaucracy's private aggrandizement, while Confucian bureaucracy, resisting such pressures, interpreted them as the monarch's moves to make the *t'ien-hsia* private, and thus to fail in moral concern for the public well-being.

Part Three

THE BREAK IN THE
LINE OF TENSION

CHAPTER VI

Bureaucracy's Long Imperviousness to Social Revolution: the Role of Confucianism

I. MONARCH AND PEOPLE

THE tension between emperor and bureaucracy was not the old order's weakness but its strength. When it ended, when Confucianism ceased to imply conflict as well as confederacy with monarchy, this was the decline of Confucianism as the specific intelligence of the Chinese world. With that decline, the bureaucracy slid all the way (or seemed so, to a fatally large mass of the people), for the first time, to utter parasitism. And a ruling class of parasites incites to revolution.

Conventional Chinese monarchy could reap no gains from this. Whatever its old interest in breaking the independence of bureaucracy, its involvement with bureaucracy was too close to give it the pleasures without the pains of the latter's devastation. The monarch tried recurrently to level away the aristocratic potential in bureaucracy, his agent against the feudal aristocracies, but he never came to identity of interest with rebels against bureaucracy from below. In their traditional attitudes toward Taoism, for example, monarchs showed, on the one hand, affinity with the public beneath bureaucracy, and yet, on the other hand, acknowledgment of the common lot of Confucianism and monarchy.

It is well known that Taoism in its religious form, which

jarred on sophisticated Confucian officials, was widely popular, and never so much as when social order (a precious state to Confucianists in particular) was menaced. Monarchs, too, had frequently shown some interest in formal, creedal Taoism (beyond its general implications for aesthetics) which Confucianists disliked—indeed, this was one of the many marks of Confucian-monarchical tension. In T'ang times, for example, an eighth-century emperor established temples to Lao-tzu and a school of Taoist studies; and the school's curriculum, with Taoist texts as its 'Five Classics', matched and rivalled the Confucianists'.[1] For in a way, Taoism was as appropriate as Legalism to the emperor's counter-Confucian interest. Just as a Legalist approach implied restraints on Confucian officialdom, so Taoism (with its doctrine of following nature, a welcome corrective to the Confucian system of fixed forms imposed on natural behaviour) appealed to emperors who longed to escape Confucian restraints. After all, even when monarchy rode hardest on Confucian officials, Confucianism almost smothered the monarch in expectations of ritual and routine.

But if the intrusion of Taoist 'Classics' on the Confucian examination syllabus was possible for monarchs, the enjoyment of Taoist rebellious effervescence was not. They were curbed by the Confucian blackmail of the 'mandate of Heaven', which made rebellions a sign, not of a popular-royal front against the literati, but of the failure of royal virtue—while the literati as a type, if not always as individuals, rode out the storm. Accordingly, the Ch'ing dynasty, for one, took great pains to bring religious sects, Taoist and others, under government supervision. Some of the discipline may have been primarily just accommodation to Confucian bias—an edict of 1740, for example, forbidding an only son to become a priest, or a provision in the Ch'ing code, the *Ta Ch'ing lü-li*, insisting that priests perform ancestor ceremonial.[2] But the imperial government was doubtless disparaging in its own right when it took note in 1754 of the likely link of Taoism (and Buddhism) with low fellows, lawless *fei* or vagabonds, when it referred to priests deluding the people and improperly fostering mingling of the sexes, when it set up controls for priests' and temples' finances and the temples' numbers and acquisitions of land. Such departments as the Ming and Ch'ing *Tao-lu ssu*, office for records of Taoist priests, were for control of the Taoists, not imperial encouragement and expression of fellow-feeling.[3]

In short, post-feudal, pre-Taiping Chinese monarchs were never so closely identified with popular causes that they could take popular violence with equanimity, as tending to curb their literati rivals; rather, what made the literati rivals, in the last analysis, was their propensity for embroiling a ruling house by goading the people to violence. (When the ruling house did its own goading, like Ch'in and Sui, the bureaucracies were least the monarch's rivals, most his tools.) In Confucian eras, the Chinese masses and monarchs lacked that intimacy which one could see in pre-revolutionary Europe. There, for example, John Ball's rising in 1381 was impelled by faith in the benevolence and omnipotence of the English King.[4] When the Paris crowd turned against the royalists in 1789, it was a novel, revolutionary departure from centuries of urban popular riots in favour of 'Church and king'.[5]

2. THE 'PARASITE' EFFECT

What finally doomed the French king was the fading of the old popular impression of him as one fulfilling the *thèse royale*, encroaching on aristocracy and straining feudal bonds. Instead, the conviction spread that the king's interests and the aristocrats' were no longer distinguishable, so that he was a target in a revolution against them, as one parasite among many. When Mirabeau wrote to Louis XVI, in 1790, to the effect that he should relax and enjoy the Revolution, he referred to the old objectives of the centralizers ('Is it not something to be done with *parlements*, with *pays d'états*, with an all-powerful priesthood, with privilege and the nobility? The modern idea of a single class of citizens on an equal footing would certainly have pleased Richelieu, since surface equality of this kind facilitates the exercise of power').[6] Alas, poor Louis—the abstract cogency of this analysis, which should have put the king quite happily on the anti-aristocratic, centralizing side, broke down historically. The very fact that the Revolution had so much to do (Mirabeau: 'Absolute government during several successive reigns could not have done as much as this one year of revolution to make good the king's authority')[7] showed that monarchy had long since lost the power to press its case, but had made an accommodation with the nobles, one which delivered the king with them to revolution. The defenders of Louis before the Convention were not statist bourgeois, but aristocrats who in earlier days had stood for their estate against the crown.[8]

In the eighteenth century, the aristocrats had come back a good way from the days of their discomfiture at the hands of Louis XIV: but to recover their potency at the cost of making Louis XVI impotent only led to their languishing again. They had a 'victory' in the 'aristocratic revolution', beginning in 1787, culminating two years later, when the Estates General, preponderantly aristocratic, had to be convened. It espoused the *thèse nobiliaire*, calling for liberty in the sense of Montesquieu—that is, the weakening of the royal power. But now it was far too late to realize the hopes of the old Fronde, which the greater Louis had crushed so long before. On the eve of the real French Revolution, aristocracy, by draining the royal power, was drying up the channel of its own privilege.[9] Louis XIV had certainly not ruined the nobles for good in his own day; but he had taken so much, made them so much a part of him, that when they took from his royal descendants they were plundering themselves.

The fatal thing about the French monarchy's accommodation to aristocracy was that it was originally achieved, first, by taking the peerage's power, and second, by leaving it with its grandiose pretensions, so that no force might unite the two and seriously compete with the king. The lure of Versailles and the dangers of staying away, together with the power of the king's ministers and *intendants*, drastically diluted the aristocratic leadership in the country. Thus the king, though starting on the revolutionary road by stripping the aristocracy of its traditional place in local life and government, failed to wipe out the aristocracy (revolution's objective); rather, he himself seemed responsible for keeping it going, binding it to himself for his own purposes, and rendering it useless, merely consumptive, hence far more inflammatory than ever.[10] By denaturing, then sponsoring the nobles, he made himself, not the patron of the public, but the grandest and most private seigneur of them all. Once they had been assimilated to his interest, he was assimilated to theirs, and to their reputation.

When the aristocrats rose from their Louis XIV nadir, the political functions they recovered (even invading the intendancies) were made for the most part into functions of patronage, not service. To the extent that nobles (that is, the court nobles, not the provincial backwoodsmen) were ready to marry rich bourgeoises, the will to consume had eaten into the old noble pride in separation, the pride of men with a fair claim to fancy themselves the conspicuous actors, not just the conspicuous eaters, in society. And at the last, their will to consume had prevented the monarch from taxing nobles to strengthen the state. Easy, automatic manorial dues were jealously defended.[11]

De Tocqueville and Taine, historians of the Old Régime, went too far in dramatizing a royal assault on aristocratic power. Adopting the *thèse nobiliaire* themselves, they wrote almost as though nothing had happened after Louis XIV to bring the nobles back, as though a despotic, royal-bureaucratic assault on freedom had reduced the nobles to permanent subservience.[12] But, though their view was distorted, and by and large the aristocracy was not weak in eighteenth-century France, its strength was strength to obstruct, to sap any central authority, but not to reinvigorate regional life, or to act constructively from Paris and Versailles, where most preferred to live. Their reputation as gentlemen—and the king's too, as the first gentleman—became the reputation of parasites. When Sieyès, in his famous revolutionary pamphlet, *What Is The Third Estate?*, called the privileged orders *useless*,[13] he confirmed at least the subjective impression of the nobles' emasculation.

3. THE IMPORTANCE OF INTELLECTUAL WORK

What was the difference between the revolutionary French situation and the pre-revolutionary Chinese? Alignments of forces in the two countries seem analogous: a monarch so situated vis-à-vis the aristocracy (or what in certain respects could pass for one) that revolts against this privileged class had to implicate him. By the respective fruits of these revolts we know that a difference existed somewhere—that is, French monarchy and aristocracy were never the same again after 1789, while Chinese monarchy and bureaucracy kept on recovering their institutional places. And this was so because one crucial factor distinguished the French and Chinese situations, making the one ultimately revolutionary, and the other perennially rebellious: Chinese nobility was so overshadowed by Confucian bureaucracy that the nobility, however useless, could not compare with the French nobility as a focal point of hostility—and Confucian bureaucrats, more nearly equivalent to the French peers as the *visible* aristocracy, had never been spoiled by the crown, never been made (at least as a public, *à la française*, might see them) into popinjays. Never, even when economically and politically they seemed most purely exploiters and least contributors, had they abdicated that last responsibility which ties potential parasites to the world of function, the responsibility of thought.

A Chinese peasantry might groan under the burden of Mencius' famous dictum (III A, iv, 6): 'Some labour with their minds, and some labour with their strength. Those who labour with their minds govern others, those who labour with their strength are governed by others. Those who are governed by others support them: those who govern others are supported by them.' But as long as the governors did indeed 'labour with their minds', as long as they maintained their occupational badge, their Confucian intelligence, as *the* intelligence of the society, they were never, as a ruling class, parasites in the full sense of the term. Chinese peasants might rebel against them, but in France, where 'parasite' was rather more appropriate, revolution came. For French aristocrats

were not only economically exploitative and politically un-
productive; they showed every sign of defecting intellectually
to the *new* intelligence of the bourgeois *philosophes*. French
aristocrats, but not Chinese, began to bear the unmistakable
stigmata of parasites, the marks of intellectual abdication.
Both the labour with strength and the labour with mind
were being done by others in France. How could a coterie
which was reduced to talk resist the charm of another which
talked so well?

In 1635 this intellectual eclipse of the French aristocracy
had been foreshadowed, even fostered, by the founding of the
Académie Française. This was the work of Richelieu, the centralizer whose grand design, as Mirabeau assumed, the
Revolution furthered. Richelieu's essential principle for the
Academy was equality. No privilege whatever should accrue
to rank, and under Richelieu no great lords were members.
Richelieu himself did not take part, but made himself the
protector of academicians, not their confrere.[14] For pride of
place in the Academy, Latin was displaced by French—the
vulgar language and the national language, anti-feudal on
both these counts. It was national, too, in its dedication to the
intellectual and religious unity of France; Richelieu approved
as initial members a number of Cartesians and Protestants.[15]
Voltaire, who was a great partisan of the *thèse royale*, opposed
to infringements on the royal prerogative, had no doubt how
to relate the *parlements*, the voices of aristocracy, to this
intellectual body. They had persistently opposed all healthy
innovations, he said, from the Academy on.[16]

This was the Academy (an appropriate instrument for the
assailant of aristocratic power) which glorified Louis XIV.
Here, as in China, we see dignity accorded to intellectual
achievement. But in France this finally gave aristocrats the
look of utter parasites, who not only dropped out of active
service but even relinquished the function of intellect to
outsiders.[17] In China, the insiders remained the intellectuals.
What preserved the quasi-aristocratic Chinese bureaucracy
from parasitism was, quite simply, the fact that unlike the
genuine aristocracy of France it had not been broken, then
preserved. Instead it kept its distance from (its tension with)

the royal power, *served* as bureaucracy, *thought* as Confucianists, never merely tripped and strutted, in the world of affairs and the world of mind, in florid impotence. Even for France, the parasite picture is overdrawn; yet, caricature though it may have been, it was spread around. It could seem believable—and this was fact—even if its patches of fiction make it unworthy of full belief.

The intellectual histories of both China and France in the eighteenth century were distinguished by great encyclopaedic efforts. One has only to quote the *philosophe*, Diderot, on (and in) the French *Encyclopédie* ('Today . . . we are beginning to shake off the yoke of authority and tradition in order to hold fast to the laws of reason . . . we dare to raise doubts about the infallibility of Aristotle and Plato. . . . The world has long awaited a reasoning age, an age when the rules would be sought no longer in the classical authors but in nature'[18]) to see how far he was from the world of the *T'u-shu chi-ch'eng*, or 'Ch'ing Encyclopaedia', and the *Ssu-ku ch'üan-shu*, the 'Four Treasuries'. The tone of the Chinese works was traditional, not rationalistically 'modern': and these greatest of eighteenth-century Chinese intellectual achievements were unimpeachably official, products of the 'establishment'. No rival, seductive party in China, in their thought and by *their* thinking it, had yet confirmed the established ones as parasites.

There were some Confucian literati who saw the spectre of parasitism in these eighteenth-century literary projects. *K'ao-cheng*, close textual study, was the vogue associated with such labours, and *k'ao-cheng* was as apolitical in its own way as Sung-school metaphysics, which the early Ch'ing scholars of the *Han-hsüeh*, the 'Han Learning', had criticized severely. The masses were said to have been drained dry in Ming times, and the dynasty's strength sapped before the Manchus, by economic exploitation which neo-Confucian quietists had done nothing to correct. Practical statesmanship, *ching-shih chih-yung*, had been the recommendation of the *Han-hsüeh* (or later, the *Kung-yang* school, after a relatively neglected, suggestive text which the *Han-hsüeh* rehabilitated). The recommendation was made in order to keep the bureaucracy functional. But textual criticism, though non-metaphysical itself, had cancelled the corrective of the excessive metaphysics.[19]

Still, however necessary such a corrective was deemed to be, the corrective was sought, by those who did seek one, within the Confucian tradition. As long as Confucian near-parasites were condemned by standards of Confucian reformism, they were not the pure parasites, utterly divorced from the sources of contemporary intellectual vitality, whom revolutionaries identified. The *Kung-yang* reformist, Wei Yüan (1794–1856), wrote, 'The princely man takes the *tao* as pleasant and sees the bitterness of desire; the small man takes desire as pleasant and sees the bitterness of tao.'[20] There is no doubt that Wei Yüan saw most of his contemporary fellow-literati as small men, *hsiao-jen*. But he still held up before them the time-honoured Confucian ideal of the princely man, the *chün-tzu*, and tried to renew the traditional intelligence. The Taipings, however, who made their bid before Wei died, threw out the old criteria, and proclaimed by their anti-Confucian, non-reformist challenge, not that there were *hsiao-jen* where *chün-tzu* ought to be, but that the title of *chün-tzu* had no honour left.

True princes, such as the noble members of the Ming imperial family, could be deemed parasites by Confucian standards and out of Confucian motives, but when 'princely men' were despised, as the Taipings were ready to do, the Confucianists themselves were sent to the wall. Taipings ceased to acknowledge that what was in the mind of those who 'laboured with their minds' was compelling enough to endow the latter with the dignity of labour. Without that grant of dignity there was nothing left but the sense of exploitation.

The Taiping indictment was not in itself sufficient to stamp the literati as parasites. They rejected the imputation, and Confucianism was still around for a final phase as the society's intelligence, a *Kung-yang* reform movement at the end of the nineteenth century. Wei Yüan's hope for the redemption of Confucianists survived, for a while, the Taipings' rejection of Confucianists *en masse*, the princely with the small. Yet, the damage was done. Though Taipings did not establish in their own day that Confucianism was finished as the intelligence of the society (and Confucian officials thus reduced to parasites), they drove Confucianism to end its tension with conventional Chinese monarchy, to lose what gave it its character, its vitality—and, in its new fatal pallor, to condemn its official exponents to the parasitical state. Proto-revolutionary Taiping rebels took the Confucian-imperial order out of the path of rebellions, and set it up for the unmistakable revolutionaries who were still to come.

CHAPTER VII

Bureaucracy's Vulnerability: the Intellectual Point of attack

I. THE NOVELTY OF THE TAIPING ASSAULT ON CONFUCIANISTS IN POWER

WHY was this rebellion different from all other rebellions? In all other rebellions such non-Confucian doctrine as the rebels held, Taoist or Buddhist in overtones, was not really a positive challenge to Confucianism as the intelligence of society; but the pseudo-Christianity of the Taipings was just such a challenge. In Taoist or Buddhist rebellions the doctrine, for the time of violence, was chiliastic —i.e., anti-social, anti-historical in the messianic sense of a vision of the 'end of days', with Confucianism left undisturbed as the dominant thought for prosaic social history. And when society struggled through the welter of violence, the Confucian arrangement with monarchy continued to govern history, while Taoism and Buddhism, losing their transitory associations with what Han 'Yellow Turbans' or Ch'ing 'White Lotus' felt almost as the 'pangs of the Messiah', resumed their low-temperature state in a continuing dynastic history. True, Taiping Christianity shared with earlier non-Confucianism movements a symbolic character, as a challenge to Confucian social superiors, a secession from the latter's intellectual world when its social cleavage seemed hopelessly sharp. Yet, for all this common character, Taiping Christianity was a new departure.

For one thing, Christianity was a really drastic break with

87

Confucianism, and Buddhism and Taoism were not, because Buddhism and Taoism were more broadly significant than Christianity in the 'normal' China. That is, Buddhism and Taoism had a wide, *extra-rebellious* existence in China. However they came to be invoked in times of stress, they had more than a pathological existence. But Christianity of the Taiping stamp was purely rebellion-bred, rebellion-nourished, with no social existence in China except as a cultural concomitant of violence. Its newness as a colouring for rebellion in China was not just a matter of chronology, of the fact that the Christian alternative to Confucianism came to China later than the others; it was a matter of kind. Taiping rebels as 'Christians' were specifically refusing to take what lay at hand, actually existing in times of peace, and only potentially convertible into rebellious energy: Taoism or Buddhism. Instead, the Taipings took something whose only life in China was lived not in peace but in paroxysm. The fate of Taiping Christianity after the fall of the Taiping state in 1864 bears this out. If this religion had any true independence of the political and social régime with which it was associated (as Taoism and Buddhism always had), we would expect to find its traces in Chinese history of the post-Taiping century. Yet, whatever the inroads Christianity made in China in these recent times, Taiping religion seems to have laid none of the groundwork. It vanished. And as the histories of Judaism and Orthodox Christianity show, this need not be the case when a religion associated with a political order sees that order destroyed.

If the Buddhist and Taoist religious challenges to Confucianism were softened both by their sufferance in normal times and their chiliastic character in times of rebellion, the Taiping deviation was consistent: just as the Taiping religion had no existence in normal times, so its character in rebellion was an equally novel feature. Taiping doctrine did not abandon history to Confucianism by imbuing itself with chiliastic fervour for the end of history. Instead it attacked Confucianism directly by proposing to make history itself. It did this by setting up a monarchy perfectly non-Confucian in its premises, a monarchy, that is, based on a transcendental

88

religious conception, diametrically opposed to the Confucian insistence on immanence. Immanent virtue, not transcendental power, was the Confucian ideal for monarchy. And so the Taiping denial of immanence (which was also the Taiping rejection of the bureaucratic intelligence) was denial of Confucianism at just the point where the latter strained against monarchical pretensions.

Thus, the very Taiping religion which was a more vivid symbol of disaffection with Confucianism than the Buddhist or Taoist religions had a more truly incompatible substance. Confucianists of that day were profoundly convinced of it; no rebellion was ever more rebelled against. The great Ch'ing loyalist and Confucianist, Tseng Kuo-fan (1811–72), saw the hitherto despised late-Ming rebels, Li Tzu-ch'eng (1605?–45) and Chang Hsien-chung (1605–47), as relatively blameless and orthodox, compared to the Taipings, and arraigned the Taipings for their assaults on Taoists and Buddhists—who ordinarily would be suspect themselves.[1]

When Li claimed the empire in 1642, he took the three characters for 'eighteen sons' (in a prophecy that eighteen sons would conquer the throne) and re-arranged them to make the single character *li*, his name.[2] This was a typical bit of Chinese magic word-play. But when the Taiping claimant, Hung Hsiu-ch'üan (1813–64), declared himself the 'Heavenly Younger Brother' (to Jesus) in a new Trinity, and 'Heavenly King' because of that, his mystic chosenness came from a world of foreign imagery. Yet, the foreignness of the root conception, in Confucian eyes, lay in more than the fact that it came from over the borders. Just as, by the touchstone of the fullest Confucian ideal, native Chinese dynasties had something metaphorically alien about them, so the ideas of native Chinese Taiping rebels were alien, too, and not only in origin.

The core of the ideology which so disturbed literati-officials like Tseng was a blasphemy against Confucian monarchical premises. Nothing betrays so well the central importance of those premises, with the tension they implied, to Confucian vitality.

2. THE CRUCIAL QUALITY OF THE CONFUCIAN DOCTRINE OF IMMANENCE

To Confucianism, what monarch could be justified in his pride of place when Confucius, the sage, had not been king? Kingship was not despised by Confucianists, but what the world saw as the king's 'position', the outer trappings (and that meant kings in history, not the ideal conception), was hardly precious when the true king in his own day was the uncrowned Confucius, a *su-wang*, a 'monarch unadorned'.[3] 'Su-wang' implied a possible separation between *wang-tao*, the Confucian ideal of the hidden royal 'way', and *wang-i*, the monarchy's statement of visible royal rank. It was the impulse to restrain this natural tendency of monarchy to be *visible* that gave point to some of Confucianism's most vital conceptions.

Inescapably, everywhere, splendour and spectacle attach themselves to monarchy. As the ultimate leader of society, and as one not to be scrutinized for human frailties (for in that case, he might not pass), a monarch requires acceptance as something more than man, something related to divinity; majesty is the visible reflection in society of a divine splendour.

But it is a special conception of divinity—the transcendental—which spectacle connotes. Just as it sets the monarch apart, so it speaks of a divine power that is truly 'other', and truly power, the combination that spells Creator. In one mediaeval Christian theory, the king was in a sense deified (just as the Roman emperor's *consecratio* was his *apotheosis*)— the inherent distinction between God and the king (God's transcendence 'by nature' over the one He makes god 'by grace') being blurred in just the crucial category, *power*: the power of the king was the power of God.[4] And glory belonged with kingdom and power, in the earthly realm as beyond it; common forms of spectacular acclamation, eulogizing militance, successively served Roman emperors and Christian godhead and Christian monarchs.[5] The injunction to 'render unto God . . .' and 'render unto Caesar . . .' did more than distinguish the spiritual realm from the temporal; it suggested analogy as much as distinction, in that *both* God

90

and Caesar must be 'rendered unto'—surrendered to. And so the royal power reflected the Highest Power. 'In his earthly being the Caesar is like every man, but in his power he has the rank of God. . . .'[6]

A creator, however (like martial values), was alien to Confucian thought, as the literati came to profess it. However much a transcendental sentiment may be recognized in popular Chinese religion or suspected in the Classics, in a perhaps irrecoverable stratum of meaning, buried far beneath the commentaries, the literati's Confucianism—certainly by Sung, the civil bureaucracy's time of fulfilment—was committed unequivocally to immanence. It was left to nineteenth-century Christians, Western and Taiping, to dwell on the shadowy classical concept of *Shang-ti* as a transcendental supreme power. The traditional Confucian sancta were all bound up in *T'ien*, Heaven, whose 'mandate' (*ming*) made rulers legitimate and committed them to virtue (not power), to the end of harmony (not creative change). *T'ien* and *Shang-ti* had different origins. *Shang-ti* was a Shang conception (though the 'Shangs' were different characters); *T'ien* came in with the conquering Chou, who spread the doctrine of the 'mandate of Heaven' to sanctify their succession.[7] And one must not be betrayed by foreign verbal associations into the equation of the Confucian concept of 'Heaven', *T'ien*, with a transcendent God, just because in Judaism, for example, Heaven (*hashamayim*, etc.) frequently occurs as a metonym for Deity seen in that transcendental light.[8] It is not some hypothetically definitive connotation of 'Heaven' which characterizes a religion, but the character of the religion which imparts the connotation.

Scholars have recently suggested that in the period of the Warring States, in the time and region of Confucianism's first emergence, the *huang* of *Huang t'ien shang ti* (sovereign heavenly emperor) had passed over into its homonym, in *Huang-ti*, the 'Yellow Emperor'.[9] What had been heavenly became a supposedly historical monarch, and the first one, thereafter, in the Confucian list of the five model sage-kings. This would represent etymologically the Confucian transfer of emphasis from the celestial to the earthly-political sphere—

a shift from a vision of transcendental power to one of the monarch as exemplar. It is significant that the implacably anti-Confucian Ch'in Shih Huang-ti, the most challenging power-monarch of them all, claimed (as an anti-traditionalist might) to surpass the ancient 'Three Huang' and 'Five Ti', and called himself Huang-ti:[10] the pre-Confucian term, with its transcendental overtones.

Philosophically, no Creator meant no 'in the beginning', hence no progressive conception of time to threaten Confucian equilibrium, or to shatter the absolute quality of the historical thought (leaning more to paradigm and example than to process and relativity) that went with it. The corollary in political theory was a Confucian ideal of an emperor radiating virtue, analogically reflecting harmony to society, not logically interfering with it to move it; he should be sympathetically stabilizing an eternal cosmos, which had never been once created, and should never be freshly tampered with by some mock-transcendental earthly ruler, acting, creating anew. Thus Han Confucianism, with its 'Five Element' theory, gave a cyclic role to emperors in a universe of cosmic interaction, where the course of nature and human events were locked together.[11] How different this was—consistently—from a transcendentalist system. Judaism, for example, which posits a Creator who never rose and never dies, developed therefore in permanent contrast to natural, cyclical cosmologies; and the cultic function of the Davidic king (on the pattern of ritual drama, the dying and rising god of nature) was severely repressed.[12]

In the *Shuo-wen*, where the *Tso-chuan* is given as *locus classicus* (cheng i cheng min), cheng[a], 'to govern', is a cognate of cheng[b], 'to adjust'. The emperor's role is government, its definition 'adjustment' of the people's transgressions and errors.[13] The assumption here is of an eternal pattern: cheng[b] is the process of restoring conformity to it. The Sung neo-Confucianist Ch'eng Hao, memorializing his emperor, saw the 'way' of Yao and Shun as the perfecting of the five social relationships, achieving adjustment to heavenly reason.[14] This is essentially the task of a silent one, a sage in concealment (the immanent is always hidden, never spectacular).

The very idea of it clashed with a real emperor's natural place as a focal point for spectacle: note, for example, Ch'ien-lung's Confucian statement of modest expectations for his receptions on tour in 1751, and his actual prompting to flamboyant extravagance.[15] And the idea of silence and concealment clashed, too, with an emperor's natural penchant for wielding power to change the world, not for emanating perpetuation of a changeless pattern.

Where God is transcendent, man tends to be seen as intrinsically morally limited, and kings as necessarily coercive (as in patristic Christian thought, where the Fall brings sin and social disorder and the need for a power-authority;[16] and as in Maimonides' philosophy, where man's distance from transcendent God is measured by the redemptive bridge of the Law that God revealed, and where kings are those who accept the dictates of lawgivers and have the power to enforce them, compelling the people to obey).[17] But the seminal Han Confucianist Tung Chung-shu (second-century B.C.), reasoning from a premise of unfallen man, man with a good nature, sees the need of a *moral* authority—an exemplar, not a coercer—whose Heavenly Mandate is not a licence to God-like power but a certification of charm. People are good and thus can be, as it were, magicked (by *li* and *yüeh*, ritual and music) into the harmony that Heaven implies; the Son of Heaven, by his being, not his doing—as a sage, not a potentate—is the one to work or waft the magic, to bend the grass (the masses) into the immanent order of Heaven. That is what he exists to do. Man's nature is perfectible but, left to itself, not perfect—'therefore Heaven sets up the king to perfect it. . . . If the (masses'?) natures were already perfect, then to what end would the king receive the mandate?'[18]

What Confucianists, then, made of monarchy was something particularly Chinese. But we can hardly understand what they made of it unless we recognize in monarchy what is potentially universal. Just what are the Confucianists doing? They are straining against the implications of un-inhibited monarchy, and to know what *those* are (and thus to know the character of Chinese history) one should look to other histories as well as to Chinese. If comparable histories yield a consistency of relations between religions and kings and bureaucracies, then in a single history (Chinese) these relations may be significant, not casual and empty.

In mediaeval European political theology, as literature and iconography show, there developed an interesting difference between Christ-centred and God-centred monarchy. Ninth-century Carolingian throne images reflect a direct relationship of God to the king as God's vice-regent; Christ is absent. But a subsequent concept of kingship, affected by a century or more of Christ-centred monastic piety, was 'liturgical' (exemplary), centred in the God-man rather than in God the Father—centred, that is, in a Christ of the Gothic age, an intimately human figure, not the regal and imperious Christ, almost *in loco Patris*, of Constantinian origins. And after that, when the christocratic-liturgical concept of kingship gave way, the theory succeeding it was theocratic again, and juristical.[19] Once more we see, as in China (and as we shall see in Byzantium), the non-Confucian, power-imperial identification with law. 'The omnipotent God is known to have set over men a king . . . that he may coerce the people subject to him by his terror, and that he may subdue them with laws for right living,' wrote a twelfth-century partisan of Emperor over Pope, setting God above Christ ('just as the head rules the body'), seeing the king in the likeness of God, and quoting St. Paul (Romans, XIII, i) with crushing imperial finality: 'Let every soul be subject to the higher powers. For there is no power but of God: the powers that be are ordained of God.'[20] This was the pretension, this drive for an unrivalled royal power, that put a divine nimbus around the heads of kings, and made the king's touch for the 'king's evil'—that derivation from God's power as the fountainhead of healing—so potentially 'Gallican' in France, so imperiously challenging and antipathetic to popes.[21]

What is the political implication of these different religious associations? It seems to be this: Whatever may have been the compulsion on Constantine, as a convert, to take his new Christ-image (not God the Father) as the heavenly antitype of the emperor on earth, Charlemagne, without the need to insist on the already accepted idea of Christ's divinity, could reach above him to the proper seat of power. Charlemagne, the centralizer, the mighty wielder of real (though transitory) power through a bureaucracy (though ephemeral) of regimented king's-men, was seen in the image of the *active* God, God the Creator, not Christ—agent, not patient. 'Sub Pontio Pilato *passus*,' the Mass declares of Christ: Christ suffered. To suffer is to be acted upon; it is God alone who acts. Truly, not king-as-Christ (ultimately a monastic, i.e., a contemplative, not an activist conception) but king-as-God (or rather, His analogue) was the appropriate image for Charlemagne, who was an ideal monarch in actively trying to break all earthly trammels. Suffering, in the deepest sense of the word, attends upon immanence. But power reflects transcendence.

This is not to say that belief in a transcendental, creative God demands the royalist analogy. John Milton, after all, believing in God, believed in the people, not the king, as the source of authority. It is interesting, though, that Milton, in visualizing King Charles I as a subject under indictment, not as a ruler enforcing law, spoke, in a way, in the Confucian vein. The fact that Charles had been defeated, imprisoned, and brought to trial was a portent to Milton, a sign of God's will that Charles be done away with[22]—a Confucianist would say, the loss of Heaven's mandate. Still, no Confucianist, before the modern rout, would have wished his monarch succeeded by a sovereign people. Milton was not so Confucian, after all, and as he worshipped a different Heaven, so he accepted a different sovereign.

God, then, need not validate king, nor the idea of God make the acceptance of kingship follow. But the logic still works the other way round: kings need God, and as kings seek power, the power of God (where divine worship is at all current) is a main on which they draw.

In the most completely austere of transcendentalisms, with idolatry under an absolute ban, the monarchical idea is basically discouraged: if God is King, there ought to be no king to play at God (see I Samuel 8: 4–7, before the enthronement of Saul in Israel). For that is surely what kingship carries with it—Deuteronomy 17: 16–20 has Moses, out of respect for God's uniqueness, vigilantly legislating modesty for kings,[23] and Mme. de Sévigné referred to Louis XIV, that lover and embodiment of spectacle, as a being compared to God in such a manner that God, not the king, was the copy.[24] Philo Judaeus of Alexandria (nothing sardonic here), accepting monarchy as Samuel had had to accept it, had seen the king as a divine simulacrum ('for there is nothing on earth that is higher than he'), administering the Law, in a world in which God is eternal king and model for human monarchs.[25] Idealistic, impersonal coinage-portraiture of Augustus expressed the idea of the *genius* or *numen*—Augustus' more than normal will, his universal and superhuman efficacy—in Greek, *daimon*, that is, *theos* viewed as an efficient agent in daily life: the impersonality of the ruler's image reflects the early Imperial Graeco-Roman religious emphasis on divine power (rather than on divine personalities).[26] In mediaeval Islam, the ruler was 'the shadow of God on earth'; the caliph or imam was 'the khalifa of Allah and the shadow of Allah who imitates the lawgiver in order to make his government perfect'.[27] The monarch in early modern Europe, unimpeded by the claims of merit, gives grace: like God (the version of Jean Calvin).[28] To the fourth century Byzantine philosopher Themistus, the ruler's primary attribute, the divine *philanthropia* (love of man), made the emperor God-like, with God's prerogative of mercy being the emperor's prerogative, too, marking for both transcendence over what they give the world—the legal codes of justice.[29] For dominant Christianity in the Byzantine Empire, this was the ground for submission to imperial authority; for dominant but very different Confucianism in China, this imperial link with formulated law, with its transcendental implications, was, we saw, a ground of conflict.

From the standpoint of Samuel's terrible warning of what a king would really mean in exercise of power (I Samuel 8: 11–18), the Byzantine's active *philanthropia* was a myth to gloss over the true potential of monarchy. From the same standpoint, the Confucian ideal of sage-like non-activity was a myth, too: the king does not stay hidden. The difference between the myths is that the Byzantine coincided with an emperor's naturally transcendental pretensions, and strengthened his hold; while the Confucian was at odds with the character of the throne, and stood as a reproach. Byzantines conceived of imperial government as a terrestrial copy of the rule of God in Heaven.[30] Confucianists had no God in Heaven, no autonomous Voice that spoke from above. In so far as monarchy inevitably approached that transcendental model, the Confucianists strained against it. They would not condemn it in the Deuteronomic, pre-Philonic Hebraic fashion, out of an utter transcendentalism unvitiated by the Greek idea of incarnation, but would correct it, as far as they could, towards silence.

Perhaps the nearest approach a Chinese emperor made to the crypto-Taoist non-activity[31] which Confucianists commended to the throne was in the imperial ineffectualness which often accompanied social breakdown. But in that case, one may be assured, there was no Confucian approval. Instead, the emperor's virtue was disparaged (usually from the safe vantage point of a later dynasty), since he had evidently not fulfilled his symbolic responsibilities as holder of Heaven's mandate. And the disparagement might be framed precisely as a charge of inactivity—*openly* labelled 'Taoist', and thus a proper object of Confucian censure.[32] Clearly, the Chinese emperor was subject to checks, material non-co-operation in his own day and at least posthumous moral reproach.

I have already suggested (in discussing 'the people's will') that these moral reproaches, for whatever they were worth, were no testimony to 'the innate democracy of Chinese political thinking'. But what still needs to be emphasized is that the immanentist *T'ien-ming* (mandate) doctrine really was an expression of conflict with the emperor (Byzantine Christian officials, much more than Chinese Confucianists, were a despot's faceless men), though a bureaucratic, not a democratic expression. (Just so, in the mediaeval European papal-royal tension, the moral challenge to monarchy—glossing over St. Paul's blanket endorsement of the 'powers that be', which was the textual underpinning of monarchical apologies—was an ecclesiastic, not a democratic challenge.)[33]

Bureaucratic historians, in their Confucian moralism, charged up to the emperor symptoms of social decay which were actually effects of the normal functioning of the bureaucracy itself.

Confucianists had to have an emperor as a reflector of morality (in social terms: officials needed a state), but by the system of morality he crowned, the emperor could be indicted to cover the part which officials played in wasting the state they needed. 'Mandate' theory was no defence of the people, mitigating absolutism, but it was a defence of gentry-literati in their conflict-collaboration with the emperor in manipulating the state.

I have no wish to imply here any organized cynicism, or conscious cabals to fool the people and bind the emperor. This is a statement of the logic of a world, not an assumption of cool detachment and logical calculation on the part of the world's leaders. What we see in the Confucian political order is an inner consistency—something not depending on the exercise of rational cunning or on any other melodrama—a consistency of intellectual theory and the intellectuals' social concerns. A conservative social group, opposed above all else to revolution while it contributes provocation to that end, favours an almost exquisitely appropriate doctrine: by making an explanation of the workings of the social system moral inner, rather than social outer, it makes the system sacrosanct and intellectually untouchable. Dynasties, the Confucianists' lightning rods to draw off the fury of social storms, go through *ko-ming*, exchanges of the mandate, but bureaucracy goes on and on, not subject to revolution.

It was subject, however, to rebellion. And Chinese bureaucracy in its characteristically Confucian form finally met its last rebellion—last, because the seeds of revolution were in it at last—with the irruption of the Taipings in 1850. All that had summed up the Confucian strain with monarchy, all the clashes in interest and taste, were intellectually gathered in the Confucian conception of Heaven, which defined (in every sense of the word) the Son of Heaven. To deny the Confucianists there was to add intellectual rejection to social hostility, and thus fill out the fatal conception of parasitism. 'French' revolution became a Chinese possibility.

Certainly, the Taipings did not rise in order to revise a definition. Their agony was social, and we may take the ideological form of the rebellion as an index of what was happening—shattering, qualitative change—not as a first cause of the change. Yet, it was some kind of a cause, too; while corollaries coincided, consequences flowed. High as they were, the clash of Heavens, immanent versus transcendent, was not just a pseudo-event in an airy 'superstructure'. The ground of Chinese history was shifting. Confucianism and monarchy would change their role in China and their posture toward each other. And the change in posture, from a bout to an embrace, decided the change in role. Confucianism and monarchy passed from expressing general reason, alive with a tense vitality, to making claims on a special Chinese emotion, but one with a dying fall.

CHAPTER VIII

Taipings Storm the Confucian Heaven

A SIXTEENTH-CENTURY German, dilating on the absolute authority of the Russian Czar, reported that the Russians conceived of their abject obedience to the will of the prince as obedience to the will of God.[1] When Hung Hsiu-ch'üan, *T'ien-wang* of the *T'ai-p'ing T'ien-kuo*, was the prince in question, he, too, took obedience to the prince as obedience to the will of God, and he was just as alien to the crucial rationalistic Confucian doctrine of 'Heaven' as any foreign divinely-mantled autocrat. When he rejected ties with certain contemporary fellow-rebels against the Ch'ing dynasty, he did so not merely because he, an aspiring monarch in his own right, could hardly share their zeal for a Ming restoration.[2] The Taiping ideal of monarchy was simply far removed from the conventional ideas of the traditional sort of rebels.

1. 'TRADITIONAL' REBELS: DIVERGENCE FROM TAIPING IDEAS

For a time in the 1850s, the shadowy figure of an Emperor T'ien-te ('Heavenly Virtue') came, in rumour, to the attention of fascinated foreign observers of a torn China. Some confused him with Hung Hsiu-ch'üan, but in fact the 'T'ien-te' manifestoes came from the circles of the *T'ien-ti hui*, 'Society of Heaven and Earth', which was also known as the Triads, and by other names as well;[3] and Hung, very early, lost any sense of common cause with them. For the Triads' assault on the Ch'ing system was such as to confirm Confucianism as the intelligence of Chinese society, while the Taipings thrust it off. The Taipings, for example, made little of filial piety. They could hardly take this Triad appeal as an acceptable piece of anti-Manchu rhetoric: 'To help an enemy to attack one's homeland is the same as leading children to attack their parents.'[4]

The secret societies reviled the Manchus, repeatedly, for 'selling office, vending noble rank' ('like Shang Yang oppressing the people'), and thus bypassing the legitimate claims of Confucian learning.[5] That is, the Manchus were equated with a Confucianist's villain (the ancient 'Legalist', Shang Yang), and Confucianists were included among the victims of parasites. But the Taipings named the Confucianists themselves in the charge against parasites, and made that charge more sweeping, because so much more inclusive. When the learned Confucianists were not the injured ones but the worthless injurers, not just the dynasty but the whole legitimate system was arraigned. And not just this dynasty but the Ming or any like it was rejected when the Confucian learning, in its application to monarchy, was explicitly supplanted, as worthless. For the 'T'ien' of *T'ien-te* was the impersonal cosmic harmony of the neo-Confucianists: 'Ta Ming T'ien-te Huang-ti *t'i T'ien hsing jen*,' a proclamation ran, 'The T'ien-te Emperor of the Great Ming *has Heaven as his essence and benevolence as his function*' (hsing = yung in the famous neo-Confucian *t'i-yung* dichotomy).[6] 'T'ien' as his essence—this 'inner' conception of the relation of monarch to the harmony of the cosmos was never the Taiping 'T'ien', which pertained to a transcendent God, whose *T'ien-ming* was personal commandment from on high, not the Confucian impersonal mark of election. Hung as *T'ien-wang* was not 'King of Heaven' (in the fashion of a Ming pretender, hopefully *T'ien-tzu*, 'Son of Heaven')—he was 'Heavenly King', a ruler receiving orders from God in Heaven, set apart, not one with Heaven 'in essence'.

The term *T'ien-wang* was not new with the Taipings. Ku Yen-wu (1613–82) discussed it as a classical term of Chou.

But only with the Taipings was *T'ien-wang* set against *T'ien-tzu* as the term for the claimant to oecumenical rule.[7]

2. TAIPING 'T'IEN' AND THE TRANSCENDENTAL AURA OF POWER

Hung Hsiu-ch'üan never maintained that the Ch'ing dynasty had lost the Mandate of Heaven. He never made this conventional rebel claim because he never thought of his own position as legitimized by the Mandate. Not 'Heaven' but 'God in Heaven' was the source of his authority, and when *T'ien-ming* appears in Taiping documents *T'ien* is, metonymously, 'God', and *ming* is 'order' in its Biblical sense of commandment, not in its Confucian sense of timeless pattern.

For the metonymy, it is sufficient to note that when Hung Jen-kan (the 'Shield King' of the Taipings) enjoined, *Ching T'ien ai jen* ('Revere Heaven and love men') he meant explicitly to quote words of Jesus,[8] whose object of reverence was what the Taipings, too, repeatedly called their 'Heavenly Father'. 'Wo T'ien-wang feng *T'ien-fu* Shang-ti chih *ming*,' declared the Taipings, 'Our Heavenly King receives the commandments of God (*Shang-ti*), the Heavenly Father (*T'ien-fu*).'[9] Clearly, on this showing, the Taiping *T'ien-ming* compound is an ellipsis: between 'T'ien' and 'ming' falls the Father-God.

It is clear, too, that just as 'Tien' signifies God for the Taipings, God who as creator brings time into the timeless, so *ming* is a different 'order' from the Confucian timeless one. How does the 'T'ien-wang' receive 'T'ien-fu Shang-ti chih ming?' *Feng* is the verb, signifying receipt from a superior, while an emperor in Confucian texts almost never receives his *T'ien-ming* thus, but with *ch'eng* or (usually) *shou*. The great Han Confucianist, Tung Chung-shu, had laid it down, 'only the Son of Heaven receives (*shou*) the *ming* from Heaven; the Empire receives the *ming* from the Son of Heaven.'[10] The *ming* so received and transmitted was an imprint of order (we have seen Tung Chung-shu allotting the monarch the role of ordering men's hearts by an example that only he can radiate). But Hung Hsiu-ch'üan 'feng T'ien-ming hsia-fan', receives the heavenly order *to come down* to earth (while Confucian *T'ien-ming* is not an order *to do* anything, and the holder, of course, is on earth already); 'feng T'ien-ming', here, has the same significance as in the subsequent phrase, '*feng Shang-ti chih ming* (receives God's order) to exterminate the goblin people . . .'[11] When the Taiping 'Heavenly Father' demands acceptance of himself, Jesus (*T'ien-hsiung*, Heavenly Elder Brother), and Hung Hsiu-ch'üan (the Heavenly King and Heavenly Younger Brother), he endorses the latter's political supremacy in this quite different fashion: 'When he utters a word it is *T'ien-ming*; you are to obey it.'[12]

This is God's injunction to men to obey the *T'ien-wang* and obey the *T'ien-ming* because God speaks the latter, His orders, through the former, His younger son. The *ming* of Confucian *T'ien-ming* could never be governed as it is here, by *tsun*, 'obey', just as the *T'ien* who 'speaks' it here could only, really, be the Taiping *T'ien-fu*, the Heavenly Father: when Confucius asked, rhetorically, 'Does Heaven speak?' he went on to identify it with the timeless cosmic pattern.[13] And so the Confucian *ming* of Heaven perennially exists, with only the qualified holders changing. But the Taiping *ming* is given in time, spoken from above, to be obeyed from below. The books of the 'true Tao' of the Taipings are given as three, Old Testament, New Testament, and *Chen T'ien-ming chao shu* (Book of the true heavenly decrees and edicts); Confucian books are daemonic, noxious, and ought to be burned.[14] Or, in sum, the 'true *T'ien-ming*' of the Taipings must be far removed from the Confucian understanding— Hung does not receive the 'mandate' because the Ch'ing have 'lost' it—for, if that were the Taipings' contention, they would appeal to the sanction of Confucian books instead of advancing a canon to supplant them. The anti-Confucian *régime* may be referred to as 'true *T'ien-ming*',[15] but the monarch, unlike a Confucian monarch, never assumes that mandate.

It was a new canon, then, enshrining the record of God who speaks. If Confucius preferred not to speak because Heaven did not speak, Hung Hsiu-ch'üan arrogated to himself an earthly version of the speech, the power, of a Heaven personified. 'Do you know that the Heavenly Father is omnipotent, omnipresent, omniscient? I know . . .'[16] ran a Taiping catechism. Over and over again the changes were rung on Shang-ti as God of power, unlimited, inexhaustible power, and sovereigns are *neng-tzu*, those of his children whom he clothes with power.[17] There is no *neng-tzu* in the Confucian vocabulary, in which *te*, virtue, the very antithesis of outer physical force, was the ideal 'power' of monarchs. Not virtue but power is what the *T'ien-wang* gets from Heaven. God is greater than his sons—God alone is *shang*, God alone is *ti* (cf. the regular dynastic emperors, all *ti* themselves), God and Jesus alone are *sheng* or 'holy', Hung Hsiu-ch'üan is only *chu*, the people's lord.[18] God, thus transcendent, routes his authority down through the Heavenly King. Obedience to him is service to God and Jesus.[19] Hung's cousin and aide, Hung Jen-kan, distinguishing between classical titles of nobility (*kung, hou, po, tzu, nan*) and the Taiping designations, calls the latter far superior. For the classical ranks, he says, were taken from the nomenclature of the family system (indeed, they are kinship terms as well as political ones), and this arrangement was confused and inelegant. But the Taiping terms are all prefixed with 'T'ien'—the capital is *T'ien-ching*, soldiers are *T'ien-ping*, officials are *T'ien-kuan*—for the *T'ien-wang's* authority derives from the *T'ien-fu*.[20]

3. SIGNIFICANCE OF THE BIBLE AS SUCCESSOR TO THE CLASSICS

These *T'ien-kuan* were supposed to be chosen for the Taiping service by an examination system, and for this traditional procedure the Taipings modified their strictures on the traditional literature. God was said to have acknowledged that Confucius and Mencius had many good points in common with divine sentiment and reason, and that the Four Books and Five Classics, *imperially revised*, their falsehoods noted, could be studied again as supplementary texts for examination candidates. But the fundamental texts were the *Chiu-yüeh*, *Ch'ien-yüeh* and *Chen-yüeh*—the Old Testament,

New Testament, and 'true testament' of Taiping decrees and edicts. [21]

A Ch'ing intelligence report on this examination system noted that the essay retained the 'eight-leg' (*pa-ku*) form, and the poem the regular Ch'ing form (*shih-t'ieh*; eight five-character lines). However, the subjects were all drawn from false books. For example, a Hupei essay was set on the theme, 'The true God (*chen-shen*) is the sole Lord (*Huang-shang-ti*)', with the next phrase, '*Huang-shang-ti* is the true emperor (*Huang-ti*)'. The poem dealt with the Incarnation and the Passion. [22] (The 'false books' are *wei-shu*. One may note in passing that wherever the Taiping documents prefix *T'ien*, this Ch'ing account prefixes *wei*, 'spurious'—*wei-ching*, *wei-ping*, *wei-kuan*, etc.—with much the same regularity and ritualistic impact as the sanguinary or conjunctive expletives of the British or American military argot.)

Does the retention of traditional forms—the examination system itself, and the form of questions—make a nullity of the shift in content? To say so would be to deny the significance of Confucian content throughout previous Chinese history, to make any intellectual content inconsequential in itself, as though it served only as a symbol of the importance of intellect in the abstract, not as serious intellectual substance. But something really significant did happen with the Taiping change from Confucian to Biblical subject matter; it was no change in 'mere form'. For just as Taiping *T'ien-ming* cut through the restraints in the Confucian conception of monarchy, Taiping examinations demanded officials' adherence to the monarch's ideology, to the books which made him legitimate. But Confucian examinations enshrined the books which made *officials* legitimate in their high places (and a monarch legitimate *in their way*), and which confirmed their grandeur, their freedom from a royal proprietor, by commanding his adherence as well, the monarch's adherence to the officials' ideology.

The T'ang monarch who in the eighth century A.D. put the Taoist 'Five Classics' on the scholars' curriculum was doubtless showing some independence of Confucian authority in the examination sphere. But the very devising of a Taoist canon of 'Five Classics' was clearly a tribute to the Confucian Classics' prestige, and the Taoist canon, tentatively put forward as rival to the Confucian, was never supposed to supersede it. Just that, however, was what the Taipings' triple testament was meant to do. The Taiping examination, far from confirming a continuity of Confucianists and Taipings, marked a rupture with the past, the displacement of the Confucian intelligence.

4. THE TAIPING RELATION TO CONFUCIANISM

In the harshest of Taiping anti-Confucian writings, Confucius is questioned and whipped before God for his deception of mankind. His books are invidiously compared with the Taiping canon, which God is said to have handed down, free of error.[23] Such a purely anti-Confucian note was not sustained. But selective borrowings from Confucian materials commonly served only to enrich iconoclastic statements. '*T'ien-hsia* (the empire, the world) is one family', 'Within the four seas all men are brothers' were statements whose antiquity the Taipings acknowledged while avowing them as their own. Yet these phrases, Confucian enough (though rather special), were adduced to support their Christian heresy: 'Your flesh is all flesh begotten by fathers and mothers, but your souls are begotten of God.'[24] Here, with this matter-spirit insinuation, we see (as in Hung Jen-kan's distinction between Taiping and classical hierarchies) a deprecation of the family.

Statements of Confucian universalism, then, were wrenched into the service of a very different, a Christian universalism (the preceding classical phrases were used in a proclamation entitled, 'Saving all God's Heaven-begotten, Heaven-nurtured children'). After declaring that God's love and his summons to bliss in heaven are available to all, all can become his sons and daughters through following his commandments, a Taiping prophet declares: 'In all the world under Heaven there shall be neither China nor barbarian (foreign) nation (*pu lun Chung-kuo fan-kuo*), neither male, nor female . . .'[25] This is 'neither Jew nor Greek' theology, and Confucianists, with their strong sense of history and culture—their own universalism bound up in the oecumenical pretensions of Chinese culture—could hardly accept this anti-historical Pauline version of universalism, with its disparagement of cultural significance.

There are words here which are words of Confucianists—*T'ien-hsia* (under Heaven), *fan-kuo* (barbarian country)—but the language is new. For while the Taipings might conclude that 'when *T'ien-hsia* is one family, *Chung-kuo* is one person',[26] Confucianists must deny this species of all-under-God equality, and take *fan-kuo* literally, as barbarian nations truly inferior to *Chung-kuo*. But the Taipings made *fan* a metaphor, with the neutral connotations of 'foreign' succeeding the primary sense of 'barbarian', inferior to China. '*Huang-shang-ti* in six days created heaven and earth and mountains and seas and men and things. *Chung-kuo* and *fan-kuo* were all together proceeding on this great road. However, each *fan-kuo* of the West has proceeded on this great road to the bottom, but *Chung-kuo*, after proceeding on this great road, then strayed on to the devil's road in the last one or two thousand years and was taken into the clutch of the daemon king of Hell.'[27] Here it is *China* which has fallen away from the highest value, while *fan* can have no offensive significance, since the *fan-kuo* have been loyal.

It has been noted[28] that the compound, *T'ai-p'ing*, comes from a text much studied in Hung Hsiu-ch'üan's home region, the *Kung-yang chuan*, key document of that Confucian reform movement which ran through scholars like Wei Yüan to its final phase in the school of K'ang Yu-wei. Just as *Kung-yang* reformers contended that China had abandoned its genuine ancient wisdom, so the Taipings insisted that in high antiquity there was only the 'true way', when the whole people worshipped God, *Huang-shang-ti*, and they culled Shang-ti references from the Classics.[29] But only the *Kung-yang* school, not the Taipings, were conceivably perpetuating the Confucian intelligence. The reformers were still Confucian enough to have their universalism begin with China; the world was held to be following a pattern of history discerned only by the prophetic Confucius. The Taipings, on the contrary, saw it as a universally shared revelation. To K'ang Yu-wei, China had fallen away from a truth, an idea of progress through history, which the Chinese sage propounded and which the West had only exemplified. To the Taipings, China had fallen away from a truth which the West had both *known* and accepted. Taipings averred, not China's particular reception of universal truth, but China's defection from the universal. And when they offered China a recovered sense of primacy, it was by exalting China as the setting of the newest revelation, elevating a contemporary Chinese to a new universal trinity.[30] Confucius, the master of the old, was not their sage, and Confucianism not the intelligence of the China they foresaw.

5. TAIPING EGALITARIANISM

Thus, though the influence of the *Kung-yang* school may have turned Taiping attention to the *Li-yün* section of the *Li-chi* (another favourite classical text of the school), the effect was not Confucian but despotically levelling in the Taipings' purest monarchical manner. A Taiping document calling all men brothers and all women sisters continued directly with, *Ta tao chih hsing yeh, T'ien-hsia wei kung*—in Legge's translation from the *Li-chi*, 'When the Grand Course was pursued, a public and common spirit ruled all under the sky.'[31] This same Taiping document which dwells on the *kung*, the public, explains the equality as deriving from the (strictly non-Confucian) universal fatherhood of God,[32] and another document, declaring that the Heavenly Father wants no inequalities, goes on to say: 'The *T'ien-hsia* is all God's one great family, the *T'ien-hsia*'s population does not receive private property.'[33] It has been remarked clearly that this levelling sentiment ran counter to the traditional vertical 'five relationships' and the 'five constant virtues'.[34]

An intelligence report on the Taipings to Tseng Kuo-fan noted the long background in Chinese history of heterodox *chiao*, religions, and their relations to class disturbances. Most recently the *T'ien-chu chiao* (Lord of Heaven religion, Christianity), repressed by officials, changed names from *chiao* to *hui*. After the English barbarians were soothed, the disobedient people of the southeast coast became more and more violent. Hung Hsiu-ch'üan and others consolidated some of the bandit *hui*, beginning as the *Shang-ti hui*, then changing the name to *T'ien-ti hui* (in either of two homophonous compounds, meaning, respectively, 'Emperor of Heaven Society' and 'Increase Younger Brothers Society'; the *T'ien-ti* of the 'Heaven and Earth Society', that *alter ego* of the Triads, does not appear in this account, but it is certainly suggestive concerning the Taipings' entanglement with the secret societies). Initiates paid no heed to seniority, and for this reason they were all 'younger brothers' thereafter.[35]

Here, in this Aesopian language of interchangeable parts, is the Taiping identification of an anti-Confucian acceptance of a transcendental God with an anti-hierarchical (hence anti-Confucian) social system. And it is linked with a feeling for monarchical supremacy which recalls the conventional straining of monarchy against hierarchical, immanentist Confucianism. 'Men should know', ran a Taiping hymn, 'that *ching-t'ien*, the reverence due to Heaven, is superior to *hsiao-ch'in*, filial obligations to parents.'[36] We can almost hear the Yung-cheng emperor here, *contra* the Sung Confucianist, Ou-yang Hsiu, insisting that an official 'gives himself to his prince, and can no longer consider himself as belonging to his father and mother'.[37] We hear him again in the voice of Hung Jen-kan, attacking 'faction', Yung-cheng's particular target. The Taiping, like the Ch'ing, rules that *p'eng-tang*, factions, cannot exist, for the *kuan* are attached to the court, as officials committed to serving the public interest, not a private one, and they must not make alliances among themselves. For a sovereign is to his ministers as a general to his subordinates: if the underlings combined, they would impair the sovereign's power.[38]

Taipings, however, were not the men to admit that a Ch'ing emperor united power with the public interest. A Taiping document proclaiming God's universal ownership excoriated the Manchus: 'The *T'ien-hsia* is *Shang-ti*'s, not the *Hu-lu*'s, the despicable northerners'.[39] Taipings saw the

Ch'ing dynasty—and any dynasty so Confucianized that it could not acknowledge, 'The earth is the Lord's' . . . as *ssu*, not *kung*, private, not public. The Taipings were no more just simple monarchists straining against a Confucian bureaucracy which nevertheless influenced them, than they were simple Confucianists, straining against a monarchy which nevertheless patronized them. This rising against Confucianists as parasites was a rising, too, against the imperial system, that traditional monarchy which, whatever its own public-private tensions with the same Confucianists, could never break them in the Taiping spirit, as the purely private purveyors of a dead intelligence—*purely* private just because the intelligence was dead.

6. PSYCHOLOGICAL REPERCUSSIONS OF THE PECULIAR TAIPING ASSAULT

Faced with a common foe, Confucianism and monarchy kept their relationship but lost their tension; the attack on both together fused their interests and thereby changed their character. The new character was one in which, ultimately, the *Chinese* associations of both Confucianism and the imperial system were stressed—Chinese, as distinct from the alien creeds and systems whose mounting influence in modern China was prefigured in the Taipings. 'Internal barbarians', the culturally heretical Taipings, had to be put down in the name of Confucian culture for *all* Chinese; Confucianism could not be acknowledged as just the weapon of a class. And external barbarians, the culturally alien westerners, had to be resisted in the name of Confucian culture for all *Chinese*. It could no longer be really conceived of as culture for the world—*T'ien-hsia*, the world as well as 'the Empire'.

For the fact that, within, Taipings had to be reckoned with meant that, without, western nations were not really barbarian any more (which is just what the Taipings implied, when they metaphorized *fan*, 'barbarian', to the morally neutral 'foreign'). Westerners, that is, could no longer be deemed barbarians in the old sense, men, perhaps recalcitrant, who yet conceivably aspired to Confucian culture, men who were potentially Chinese though handicapped by distance from the centre of the world. Instead, they were genuine rivals, able, obviously, to pose cultural alternatives even to Chinese; for they had made the Taipings, *and hence the Confucianists,* culturally equivocal. And so the demands of Chinese identity, not the claim of universality, came to dominate the world of Chinese thought and institutions. All tension spent, a twentieth-century Confucianism, entangled with monarchy in a 'national spirit' traditionalism, departed from the original, the tension-ridden tradition, to which it yearned back.

It must be said again: Confucianism ceased to tense against monarchy because the Taipings stabbed it at the point ('Heaven') where the tension expressed itself. It was this that made the Taipings irredeemable foes. Taiping religion, in its transcendentalist attack on Confucian 'T'ien-ming' immanence, denied Confucianism just where it declared its peculiar freedom, where the Confucian official refused to concede the monarch's right to make him a tool; Confucian 'Heaven' belonged in a culture which elevated the amateur. But Taiping 'Heaven' blotted out the amateur ideal, and in two ways. For Taiping Christianity was a harbinger of science, which menaced Confucian amateurs culturally, just as Taiping Christianity (with its *Shang-ti* versus *T'ien*) menaced Confucian amateurs politically. The values of science (see Volume One) were specialist, impersonal, anti-traditionalist—everything incompatible with the purport of Confucianism. And so, in relation not only to power but to cultural tone, Taiping religion beat against Confucianism. The religion was shattered, but it made its impression.

In the twentieth century, anti-Confucian advocates of science have often been anti-Christian as well. Christianity, taken as the adversary of science, seemed to them a kind of ballast to throw out, to right the national balance when Confucianism, as the victim of science, had also been dismissed. But, for the Taipings, anti-Confucian without tears, Christianity seemed the ally of science against Confucian culture, not the fellow-victim of science, paired with

Confucianism. Hung Jen-kan denounced idolatry and related superstitions, and he offered Christianity as the antidote. He rejected the worship of wood and stone on the grounds of its connection with wrong-headed judgments like this: 'When there is sickness they do not call it disequilibrium of blood and "ch'i", but call it a calamity made by daemons.'[40] The medical doctrine was quaint, but the premise was naturalistic. Thus, because idolatrous superstition seemed a foe they shared ('my enemy's enemy . . .') transcendentalist religion commended science (of a sort) to the Taipings. And science, under Christian auspices or any other, was out of harmony with Confucianism—like the Taiping brand of monarchy under (a sort of) Christianity.

A taste for science meant a taste for western technology. This meant, in turn, that Taiping approval of western techniques (along with religious motifs) might implant a successor to Confucian values, not just a material supplement. And this accounts for the heavy late-Confucian investment in the *Chineseness* of Confucianism, eternal and inexpungeable and admitting of no successor, even when—naturally when— Confucian 'self-strengtheners' themselves were selling some of the pass to the West. It was not the West solely in itself that wrought a change in the essence of Confucianism; it was the West at one remove, seen through the dark glass of Taiping ideology. For that showed the threat of apostasy within the Chinese world, and heightened the passion (while warping the credo) of the true Confucian believer.

In short, when the Taipings attacked Confucian bureaucracy as intellectually hollow, more than just socially corrupt, the attack proceeded from a self-confirming premise. For the Taipings defected from Ch'ing (an action which, by itself, Confucianists could contemplate) in a spirit that flouted Confucianists as well. And because the Taipings were, not foreign assailants, but Chinese, Confucianism became *just* Chinese, like the monarchy—too much alike for the two to sustain each other, in a Chinese world narrower now than Confucianism assumed.

If Confucianism was forced into this condition, in which it lost its standing as the creative intelligence of Chinese society, and yet remained on high with the gentry-officials—what was it? Whatever it had been before, the Taipings' vision made it what they saw, ideology, its character as general idea yielding to the idea of its class character. Confucianism was compromised by the rebellion, which made it seem the cultural cloak of gentry domination, interposed against iconoclastic, nationalistic levellers. Class analysis of Confucianism was a communist inheritance from the Taipings.

The Taipings' chances for victory in their own day, as traditional rebels, were spoiled by their proto-revolutionary novelty; Confucianists were still vital enough to make their alienation from the Taiping cause fatal to it. But because of what the alienation exacted of Confucianism, Confucian vitality was drained at last, and revolution came. It took time, almost a century, for this to happen conclusively. The 1860s 'T'ung-chih Restoration' of hopeful monarchy and Confucian bureaucracy was still 'traditional'. It was not yet traditionalistic and abortive, like the mediaevalist Restoration of the 'Ultras' in France after Napoleon's fall (and Louis XVIII's death)—or the restorations in the Chinese Republican era.[41] The very violence of the Rebellion, the terrible wounds it dealt society, obscured, at first, the Confucian fate. Just because the Taipings had so ruthlessly challenged Confucianism, the latter could still be taken as an antidote, the age-old concentrate of civilization, to be swallowed again after the sickening years of anarchy. For a while, it was helpful to Confucianism to be *not* something— Taiping and outlandish. For another while, it was mildly helpful to be something—familiarly Chinese, not western.

But a body of thought, finally, has to command intellectual assent. Confucianism had to have meaningful applications, not just pleasant associations. Already thin, it has been blown over by the communist revolutionaries, who followed the Taipings in relegating Confucianism historically to a class, thus stripping it intellectually of general authority. It was not doctrine that the communists owed to the Taipings; that came straight from Marxist sources. But the doctrine reflected the Taipings'. And it was able to reflect it because the Taipings did enough damage to make the analysis plausible. As the new society measured work, Confucianists were failing to labour even with their minds. The Taiping indictment had conjured up the basis for their charge.

7. THE DIVORCE BETWEEN CONFUCIANISM AND BUREAU-CRATIC ACTION

From the 1860s on, Confucian-western syncretisms began to fill intellectual life. Though these were in the province of reformers, not anti-Confucian revolutionaries, they drastically diluted Confucianism's authority—in spite of, and because of, the syncretists' insistence that Confucian learning was the core of Chinese being. The old *nei-wai* tension, inner and outer, vanished from within Confucianism when Confucianism *en bloc* became *nei* and *t'i*, inner essence, the Chinese learning which 'western' learning should 'supplement'.[42]

And this very transformation that made Confucianism intellectually banal, all inner instead of inner-outer, made it socially ineffective. It became more and more a fetish for sentimentalists, something removed from the field of bureaucratic action—and thus not only lacking the intra-Confucian tension, but lacking, too, in consequence, external tension with monarchy. Confucianism's relation with officialdom (while imperial China lasted, and any relation lasted) came to consist of officials' concern to defend Confucianism, from the outside, as it were. This was vastly different from the authentic relation, where bureaucratic action was presumed to be inferred from Confucianism itself.

Along with the dilution of Confucian authority in the wider world, there went an inflation of Confucius' authority within Confucianism. This was no less enfeebling. The *Kung-yang* school, last of the Confucian schools, tried to provide reformist Confucian social correctives where the Taipings were revolutionary and heretical. It ended up with a Confucius so mystically prophetic, so little the guide to practical statecraft, that its proponents, appropriately, lost their bureaucratic tie and finished as politically impoverished fantasts, lacking the old institutional basis for Confucian-monarchical tension. Liao P'ing (1852–1932), envisaging his

T'ai-p'ing age, in the *Kung-yang* prophetic vein, as the time when men might levitate,[43] brought a fitting, futile denouement to the classically earthbound, socially 'engaged', politically embroiled Confucian tradition. Bureaucracy continued—though sputtering—in the late Ch'ing and Republic, but with less and less connection with Confucianism.

When the examination system was abolished in 1905, Confucian learning became pure indeed, no longer useful in a regular way for official qualifications. But Confucianism needed the dross of involvement, the examination tie, in spite of the risk of formula and rote. Of course, the idea of the non-government scholar was an old one. But voluntary retirement, in earlier times, was often still conceivably a political act. In the healthy, Han Yü type of Confucian tradition, the point of retirement was to criticize government by abstention and so improve it. But in the twentieth century, even before the monarchy fell (and a sure sign that it would stay fallen), the Confucianist out of office took his learning with him, while the Confucianist still in office did his learning on his own time. This was more than non-participation—it was the end of the Confucian tie between knowledge and action, Confucian knowledge (*t'i*) and official action (*yung*). The old order was not being renewed. Deprived of the outlet in action, the knowledge itself was not the same.

The post-Confucian communist autocracy has a bureaucratic instrument; but when Confucianism was a live intelligence, the Confucian bureaucracy was never a dead tool. The communist cadre is only a worker, replaceable at any moment (Lenin: *The State and Revolution*),[44] instead of being the superior man, who is 'not a utensil' (Confucius: *Lun-yü*, 'The Analects'). True, both these pretensions sound a little hollow, given the facts. Confucian bureaucrats, after all, were often made utensils and were easily replaced; communist bureaucrats have to strain to keep their humilities from slipping. But these are not the only facts. Official pretensions are facts, too, and they will not permit distinctions to be blurred. Confucianists and communists do not come out identical. Taipings (and other moderns) did not fail to leave their marks.

Today, Chinese bureaucracy cannot be self-centred in the old ambiguous Confucian way. In the Han dynasty, Confucianism was 'established' by the state. Now Marxism is established—but not in the spirit of *concession*. For the state now has what would-be Legalist monarchs in the old days lacked, technological means for concentrating power. And this same modern technology that builds up politically the Legalist element of the old amalgam, breaks down culturally the Confucian element.

In the contemporary scene, with the new technology at the government's disposal, no private power, like aristocracy, can parallel the sovereign as a frame for a vital centre, a privileged and trammelled bureaucracy, which radiates to both. And the new bureaucracy, unlike the old—the professional scientism of the new diverging sharply from the non-specialized humanism of the old—can hardly dwell on itself as the end and joy of man's desiring.

Part Four

THE VESTIGE
OF SUGGESTIVENESS:
CONFUCIANISM AND
MONARCHY AT THE
LAST (II)

CHAPTER IX

The Making of an Anachronism

I. THE NAME AND NATURE OF REVOLUTION

BUREAUCRACY without Confucianism—Confucianism without bureaucracy—Confucianism's intellectual content had profoundly altered. When a school of thought persists outside its familiar matrix, does this prove its vitality or its emptiness? Burckhardt, referring to Orthodox Christianity after the fall of the Byzantine Empire, which had been so intimately bound up with it, left this question open.[1] With Confucianism, it seems, the issue is less in doubt. For revolution had at last intervened in modern Chinese history, putting an end to bureaucracy's long imperviousness to the *ko-ming*, mandate-changing, of the old monarchical system. And the literal meaning of Confucian language was shaken.

When revolution came in 1911 and 1912, establishing the Republic, its participants called it *ko-ming*. But was it the same old term? It seems rather a translation back into Chinese, as it were, of the modern Japanese *kakumei* (the Japanese reading of the *ko-ming* characters) which had used the 'mandate' characters metaphorically to convey the idea of revolution. It could have been nothing but metaphor in Japan, where a monarchist theory stressing descent, not heavenly election, genealogical qualifications, not moral ones, had never been Confucian.

For the primordial heroes in Confucian myth are men, not gods or descendants of gods; but the Japanese myth begins with the sun-goddess and her Japanese warrior-offspring. Thus a Chinese monarch is legitimate when he repeats the

119

example of sage-kings of independent lineage, while a Japanese monarch is legitimate when he descends from divinity, which bequeaths his line eternity; *his* mandate is irrevocable. Only for China was Tung Chung-shu, the great Han Confucianist, really comprehensible: 'Therefore, with royalty, there is the *name* of changing régimes, there is not the *fact* of revising the Tao.'[2] The really eternal Way, that is, underlies kingship, not any particular line of kings.

Joseph de Maistre, the French Restoration royalist and ultramontane, had a quite non-Confucian transcendental religious standpoint: kings were related to God through Popes, who were entrusted by God with the education of sovereigns. And de Maistre had the Japanese, non-Chinese, reliance on genealogy. He held the Confucian-sounding opinion that in order to reign it is necessary to be already royal. Yet, de Maistre had in mind no Confucian rectification of names, no Chinese sort of suggestion that a merely *politically* legitimate king might be morally illegitimate. Like the Japanese, he made political legitimacy central, and believed that royal qualities depended on royal birth:[3] Any force that supplanted in power a genealogically qualified monarch was the force of revolution, with no legitimate 'change of mandate' about it. Thus, change of mandate, which a Chinese Confucianist could contemplate with equanimity, as a perpetuation of legitimacy, could not be reconciled with monarchical systems like European or Japanese, where the moralism of an immanent Heaven-concept paled before the inherited right of the transcendentally graced. One of the most highly esteemed of Ming writings published in Japan (Hsieh Chao-chi [chin-shih 1593], *Wu tsa tsu* ['The Five Assorted Vessels', there being five sections, on heaven, earth, man, objects, and events]) had its passages from Mencius deleted; as a modern scholar explains it, the *ko-ming* conception was thought inappropriate to the Japanese form of state.[4] (It is noteworthy that in China, too, in Ming times, Mencius was expurgated—by the founding monarch, Hung-wu, who also felt a dynast's revulsion from moralistic restraints.)[5]

Ko-ming, then, had no natural place in the Japanese

vocabulary as long as its literal Confucian sense, which was nonsense in Japan, was the only sense it had. But when modern Japan, in her foreign borrowings, moved from Chinese to western influences, and enlarged her vocabulary to encompass western ideas, the *ko-ming* compound had enough flavour of sharp political break to be assigned the meaning of revolution. Modern Chinese enlarged their vocabulary in their turn, and found in the modern Japanese language a repository of modern terms in characters. When they reached for 'revolution', they took *ko-ming*, and made the same transformation, from literal to figurative. Sun Yat-sen accepted himself as leader of a *ko-ming tang* only when (1895) in a flash of revelation of new meaning in the old term, he read in a Kobe newspaper that that was what he was: 'We saw the characters "Chung-kuo ko-ming tang Sun Yat-sen". . . . Hitherto our cast of mind had been such as to consider *ko-ming* something applying to the will to act as emperor, with our movement only to be considered as rebelling against this. From the time we saw this newspaper, we had the picture of the three characters *ko-ming tang* imprinted on our minds.'[6]

And not just Sun, who favoured revolution, but avowed traditionalists acknowledged by their usage that *ko-ming* had been captured by the moderns. In 1913, after the republican deluge, a follower of K'ang Yu-wei related *ko-ming* to Cromwell, the French Revolution, Belgian, Italian, and Swiss risings, and noted with Confucian disgust that in those *ko-ming* sons attacked their brothers and parents.[7] K'ang himself, in the same year, made an even more interesting acknowledgement of a metaphorical turning. He wrote that a '*T'ang Wu ko-ming*' (i.e., change of mandate in the Hsia-to-Shang and Shang-to-Chou fashion) was an ordinary thing in China. This was to change a dynasty's mandate, to *ko* a dynasty's *ming*. How different it was from *ko*-ing the age-old *ming* of China! Now, with the founding of the Republic, there was cultural *ko-ming*, the overthrow of historical political principles, laws, customs, morality, and the national soul: a great disaster.[8] And K'ang might have added, on his own showing, the overthrow of traditional meanings. For he accepted *ko-ming* as applying now, with an air of sad finality, to something apart from a dynasty's virtue—to the nation's very 'essence'.

It was not only the *ko-ming* which had changed its connotation. When Sun accepted the *tang*, too (as in *Ko-ming tang*, or 'Revolutionary Party'), he was talking revolution figuratively as well as literally. For the connotations of *tang* were really anti-ideological in the old monarchical world. The associations of *p'eng-tang*, 'friends' ' *tang*, personal clique or faction, were hard to shake. But *tang* now, as 'party', a modern political vehicle (or so it was hoped) for men who intended to break an old consensus, was a transformed concept—like its fellow, *ko-ming*, whose transformation had made it into nothing less than the call for transformation.

The phrase was not stripped of its old associations, its historical depth was recognized. But this very recognition reduced an ancient Confucian concept to something quaint and 'period'. For a modern, to say that Hsüan-t'ung 'lost the mandate' in 1911 was to strive with conscious anachronism for allusive effect. Once-serious Confucian content was turned into rhetoric.

The plain fact was that when *ko-ming* finished the Ch'ing it was Chinese ousting Manchus, not dynasty ousting dynasty— hence, it was Republic ousting Empire, in revolution, not in 'mandate' continuity. What could be more republican, more revolutionary, than the nationalists' slogan in late imperial times, 'fan Ch'ing fu Han', 'oppose the Ch'ing, restore the Chinese'[9]—not 'fan *Man* (Manchu) fu Han', which would have been a consistent ethnic confrontation in a more traditional age, or 'fan Ch'ing fu *Ming*', for a similar balance of dynasties. Instead of these, 'Ch'ing' (a dynasty) stood for 'Man' (a people), and the Chinese monarchical name, though culturally earned, was no protection against the ethno-national emphasis of Chinese anti-monarchists.

The violently anti-Manchu Chang Ping-lin (1868–1936), for all his cultural conservatism (see Volume One), was a republican opponent of the Ch'ing. 'Sweeping out the Manchus,' he wrote in Sun's organ, *Min-pao* (#16), 'is sweeping out the aggressor race; sweeping out Ch'ing rule is sweeping out the royal sway.'[10] There was no help for monarchy; its mystique was waning with its feeble last exponents.

Yang Tu, the foremost among Yüan Shih-k'ai's 'six martyrs', had once, without turning republican, turned away from the pro-Ch'ing *Pao-huang hui* (Protect-the-emperor society) of K'ang Yu-wei. Yang Tu sought a 'chen-ming T'ien-tzu', a son of Heaven with the true mandate.[11] But it was too late for that. He found, incredibly, Yüan Shih-k'ai. And Yüan, the Hung-hsien Emperor, buckling on his virtue where the Ch'ing had dropped it, denying the anti-traditional purport of the republicans' *ko-ming*, was an anachronism, a farceur, a period piece come to life. There was travesty, not just mis-statement, in this paean to his glory: '. . . Now the hundred names in swelling chorus sing the virtue of the (raised characters) monarch. His ministers (legs and arms) are upright and good. The general state of affairs is tranquillity and peace.'[12]

It was a starved life and it had to be. The royal latecomer was forced to look back to a sacred past, in which his brand of traditionalism and his Confucian supporters', unfortunately, was not prefigured, and in which Confucian support for monarchy, anyway, was not so straightforward. How could 'the spirit of the people', the basis of traditionalism for modern monarchists and modern Confucianists, have any place in the earlier Chinese complex, in which a foreign dynasty, patently unassimilable to the 'spirit' of the Chinese people, was always, nevertheless, an orthodox possibility? And where was the old tension between literati-Confucian traditionalism and essentially Legalist, anti-traditionalist dynastic monarchy, whether Chinese or foreign? In the great imperial ages some Confucian ideals, sacrificed in practice to the need for accommodation with the throne, had remained in force implicitly as restraints on imperial power, while *mutatis mutandis*, the same may be said on the other side. But now, revolutionaries were occasionally helping themselves to some of the old Confucian specifics against the pretensions of the throne; Yao and Shun, for example, once Confucian exhibits of virtue *versus* mere imperial descent, could now be the pride of democrats, as anti-dynastic.[13] And therefore such moral checks, after such a revolutionary take-over, had to be relinquished by surviving Confucian monarchists (though not by Confucianists who were defeatist about monarchy and tried to make a place in the Republic).[14] Now the old tension was released. Yet it was a release that brought only the rest of death, as a wraith-like monarchy and a wraith-like Confucianism faded into a final association, untroubled at last by each other, but untroubled, also, by very much of life.

2. FORM AND CONTENT

Thus, the apparent emptiness of the Chinese Republic did nothing for monarchy. The monarchical symbols were just as thoroughly drained, and this in itself reminds us that the new form of republican China was not only form but content. The Republic was really new, and *sui generis* in Chinese history—no matter what may be said, sceptically, about a carry-over of the Ch'ing system, with only the titles changed.[15]

A Confucianist in 1918, trying to make a home for Confucius in the Republic, depended on such an assertion that only names were changing. The *chün-ch'en* (prince-minister) relation, he soothingly observed, was simply a general formula to give the state a head. *Ta huang-ti* (Emperor) or *Ta tsung-t'ung* (President), what did it matter? There was still, under the Republic, a valid field for eternal Confucian relationships.[16] But the reasoning is circular: the form of state is inessential, Republic equals Empire, because the sole essential is Confucian content, which underlies inconsequential form. Or—Confucianism is central because it is central; if Confucianism were known to be lost, Confucianists could hardly maintain that 'only form' had changed.

The institution of monarchy was of just as much consequence as the philosophy (or religion) of Confucianism. When monarchy was literally lost, it was not figuratively regained. The early republican period should not be viewed as just one more warlord pendant to an imperial era, with the Nanking government of Chiang Kai-shek as the Ch'in or Sui type of abortive régime, uniting the Empire and preparing the way for a more lasting dynasty.[17] If, by traditional standards, the Hung-hsien movement was monarchical in form only (because its justifications and associations had to be new), the Republic could not be monarchical 'in all but form'.

The swift descent from revolution to a politics of faction made the Republic seem meaningless. But the expectation of meaning, even though disappointed, supplied meaning. It signified that the world of cliques, the accepted, familiar world of Confucian politics, was at last unacceptable—no longer just to emperors, but to new men from below. For new culture, with the Republic its symbol, was dissolving the familiar Confucianism; and there was a new political order, even if honoured solely in the breach.

Radical depreciation of the significance of 'form' in comparison with 'content' (a depreciation involved in suggestions that things are 'really' the same as ever in what is merely formally the Republican era in Chinese history) is both trite and misleading. If form has any 'mereness', it is not in its unimportance when it changes; it is in its failure to hold a specific content when it, form, remains the same. The forces which revised the content of monarchy likewise made the Republic more than superficially new. *Plus c'est la même chose, plus ça change*: if Yüan Shih-k'ai was a parodist as Emperor, he was not 'in essence' Emperor as President.

What was really involved in Yüan's effort to reinstate *ch'en* as the word for 'official' in his reign? There was the simple fact of its monarchical affinities, of course: there were the classic pairs of *chün* and *ch'en*, prince and minister, a relationship found in such famous catalogues as the *Tso-chuan*'s 'six *shun*' and 'ten *li*', the *Li-chi*'s 'ten *i*' and 'seven *chiao*';[18] and *wang* and *ch'en*, monarch and minister, bound together as firmly as the *Ch'un-ch'iu* and *Tso-chuan*, for of the two reputed authors, when Confucius was called a *su-wang*, Tso Ch'iu-ming was a *su-ch'en*.[19] But there was something more deeply significant about *ch'en* than any merely verbal associations. It was something relating not just to monarchy but to the cultural air of Confucian, imperial China, so that its banishment from the Republic (and consequently, Yüan's effort to restore it) symbolized a genuine change of social and intellectual climate.

Kuan, the Republic's term for official which Yüan wished to displace, was a very old one, too, but in the pre-Republican Confucian bureaucratic world it had a sense quite distinguishable from *ch'en*. *Kuan* denoted the bureaucrat in his technical, functional, impersonal capacity. It had no connection with personal cultural dignity and individuality. For example, *kuan-t'ien*, set apart from *min-t'ien* in the Ming tax system,[20] was not 'officials' land', the land of officials as persons; it was 'official land', i.e., public land as opposed to private. *Kuan* suggests the state apparatus and *min*, here, the private sector. If 'people' and 'official' were being counterposed as human types, 'official' would be *ch'en*.

For the outstanding attribute of *ch'en* (and this made it a 'grander' word) was personal status, free of technical, professional connotations. Not the task but the personal tie defined him: 'The loyal *ch'en* does not serve two princes.'[21] An official was *kuan* in his job, something akin to being a tool, a means—and *ch'en* in his position, an end.

One of the outstanding, all-pervasive values of Confucian culture, as we have seen, was its anti-professionalism. The Confucian ideal of personal cultivation was a humanistic amateurism, and Confucian education, perhaps supreme in the world for anti-vocational classicism, produced an imperial bureaucracy, accordingly, in which human relations counted for more than the network of abstract assignments (just as in Confucian society generally, human relations counted for more than legal relations). In these respects—not by accident—it differed from bureaucracies of the modern industrial West and, at least in conception, from that of the Chinese Republic. A comparison of the Ch'ing dynasty's *mu-liao* or *mu-yu* and the Republic's *k'o-chang mi-shu* may be illustrative. All these designations, on both sides of the great divide, applied to the private secretary-advisers of administrative heads. There was nothing fundamentally dissimilar in their roles, but there was a great difference in their relationships with their respective seniors and in their legal positions: the Republic's secretary-adviser was formally an official (*kuan-li*); his Ch'ing counter-part was the official's friend and technically not attached to the *pu*, the office, or paid from the public granaries.[22] As Chang Chien, a modern-minded industrialist (and later one of Yüan's supporters, though with misgivings and out of old friendship, not out of archaism) caustically observed, all Ch'ing officials, provincial and local, could appoint their own assistants, as in the Han and T'ang *mu-chih*, government by staffs of intimates.[23]

The Republican emphasis on *kuan*, then, to the exclusion of *ch'en*, was the mark of a specifically modern commitment, to a professionalized, anti-literati world in which science, industry, and the idea of progress (all of them having impersonal, hence un-Confucian, implications) claimed first attention. This was not just the preference of a faction. It was really the world which for some time had been making over and taking over China, not only manufacturing icono-clasts but transforming traditionalists. The *ch'en*, the non-specialized free man of high culture as the master-creation of civilization, who relegated to the *kuan* category the 'jobs', the 'business' of government (necessary even in the old régime, of course, but faintly unsavoury, more the price paid than the prize won with prestige), was a figure of the irredeemable past. The Republic of *kuan* meant a genuine change from the Empire of *kuan* and *ch'en*.

The Empire dissolved in *ko-ming*. *Ko-ming*, itself drained of its traditional literal meaning and metaphorized into modern 'revolution', freed men's minds and made them aware of the changing content of Chinese civilization. Chinese imperial forms became anachronisms. And *ch'en*, one of them, had its meaning changed like the *ko-ming* that had destroyed its proper world.

For *ch'en*, as was earlier suggested, had been paired not only with *kuan*, but in the Ch'ing dynasty with *nu*, 'slave'. *Nu* was the term for Manchu officials, relating them to the Ch'ing as Manchu monarchs, while the Ch'ing as Chinese emperors left Chinese officials the Confucian status of *ch'en*, in the classically noble relationship of minister to throne. Revolutionary republicanism, however, extended the application of the term 'slave', and in this way, too, marked the obliteration of the world of *ch'en*. By doctrinaire republicans, 'slave' was stripped of its literal, technical significance (which it had had for the Manchu officials, who were *nu* in a juridical sense, for all that their use of the term may seem to be simple etiquette) and made expressive, metaphorically, of all subjects of supreme monarchs. As the republican minister, Wu T'ing-fang, put it in 1912, in a placatory cable to Mongol princes, all had suffered the bitterness of slaves under the Ch'ing crown—Chinese, Manchus, Mongols, Moslems, Tibetans—and all would be brothers in the one great republic.[24] From the republican standpoint, then, to have been *ch'en* was not to have distinguished oneself from slaves but to have been a slave. For there was no *ch'en* without his *wang* or *chün*, no Confucian gentleman outside a realm—at least an ideal one, however much the real one may have strained against Confucianism. (Confucianists *had* required the Empire, even if they execrated Ch'in Shih Huang-ti.) *Ko-ming* as change of mandate would have struck off *nu* (Manchu officials) and left *ch'en* (Chinese officials) in a continuing imperial bureaucracy. But the *ko-ming* revolution, anti-imperial in more than form, retroactively confounded *ch'en* and *nu*, struck them off together, and in this alone set a seal on the end of the Empire.

Nevertheless, just as for Mao Tse-tung and his régime today, so for Yüan Shih-k'ai in his lifetime (and the same issue is at stake: changing content behind changing form, or not?), some contemporaries saw analogies with the old monarchical past. A Japanese observer in 1914, Sakamaki Teiichirō, fixed Yüan as the Wang Mang in a late version of the fall of the Former Han. Yüan, as rumour had it, was implicated in the death of the Emperor Kuang-hsü (1908), just as Wang Mang was involved in the murder of the Emperor P'ing. Subsequently, Yüan's manoeuvre to transfer power from the young successor of Kuang-hsü to himself was exactly the story of Wang Mang and the Emperor P'ing's successor. Yüan's *Chung hua min-kuo*, to sum up, stood in the same relation to regular dynastic history as the *Hsin-kuo* of Wang Mang.[25]

That was what Ch'ing loyalists thought, too—Yüan was a Wang Mang or a Ts'ao Ts'ao, depending on whether one cursed him with a Former Han or a Latter Han analogy. Yüan himself was conscious of the sinister parallel which the public was tempted to draw. In late 1911, with an open acknowledgement of the Han reference sure to be in the mind of any Chinese with a spot of malice in his historical sensitivity, Yüan had pledged himself to protect 'the infant and the widow' (P'u-i and his Empress-dowager mother): the popular designation of the last unfortunates of the Former Han. He later maintained (while trying to quash premature rumours of his ultimate ambition) that the Ch'ing had offered to yield in his favour when the revolution began, but that he was not the sort of man to violate the canons of *jen* and *i*.[26]

Two of Yüan's puppets (one of them his 'sworn brother' Hsü Shih-ch'ang, who had been brought up by Yüan's great-uncle, Yüan Chia-san) became 'Grand Guardians of the Emperor' in November, 1911, after the Prince Regent retired.[27] Suspicion grew that Yüan, in imperial fashion, was easing out the Ch'ing. There is a note of innuendo in some of Sun Yat-sen's expressions in late January, 1912, when Yüan was proceeding, in sweet independence of the Nanking Kuomintang, to set up a government in Peking, a city Sun feared for its imperial associations.[28] 'No one knows whether this provisional government is to be monarchical or republican,' said Sun on January 20. 'Yüan not only specifically injures the Republic, but is in fact an enemy of the Ch'ing emperor,' said Wu T'ing-fang, at Sun's direction, on January 28.[29] By 1913, though Yüan had crowned the occasion of the Ch'ing abdication in February 1912 with a statement that monarchy would never again function in China[30] (and Sun himself, whistling past the graveyard, had echoed this assurance as he yielded the president's office to Yüan),[31] Sun was sure that Yüan was imperial as well as imperious. The very term 'Second Revolution' for the Kiangsi rising in the summer of that year had anti-monarchical

129

overtones, and Sun's provocative public cable to a number of addressees, on July 18, read Yüan out of the Republic, right back to the ranks of Chinese absolute monarchs. Public servants, said Sun, should be subject to the people's approval. This was the case even in constitutional monarchies—how much more should it be so in a republic.[32]

3. VESTIGIAL MONARCHIES AND THE MEANING OF JAPANESE SPONSORSHIP

Yet, despite the pedantic or polemical impulses of the moment which moved men to interpret Yüan's republic as a monarchical régime, Yüan himself knew that his republic was not his empire—knew it emotionally, at the level of desire for an emperor's baubles and trappings, and knew it intellectually, at the level of tactics, in his grasp of the need to shift his base of support. Nationalism, with its iconoclastic implications, was the Republic's grain of novelty. As at least the ostensible exponent of the nation's cause against Japan in the 1915 crisis of the 'Twenty-one Demands', Yüan, the president, had the most solid public support of his life. But immediately thereafter Yüan was a would-be emperor, and he tried to feel his way to Japanese support. It was a logical effort. He was searching for something to replace the nationalists' backing. For this had been available to him as a nationalistic president, but it would necessarily be withdrawn from a traditionalistic emperor.

Yüan failed to get useful Japanese help. He had first come to Japanese attention, after all, as the main defender of the Chinese interest in Korea in the 1880s and early 1890s, and subsequently he was assumed to be playing off Westerners (or playing their game) against Japan. He was thus too old a foe of Japanese diplomacy to be rehabilitated in that quarter overnight, and his imperial chances, it was soon apparent, were too dim to convert him at the last into a likely protégé. Given the Japanese aims in China, and Yüan's reputation and self-advertisement, for so many years, as China's strong man, Japanese leaders naturally found their habit of hostility to Yüan hard to break. Certainly, to the extent that Chinese opposition to Yüan might lead to anti-national regionalist fragmentation, the care and feeding of his opponents was at least plausible for Japan.[33]

It was not surprising, then, that Japanese 'volunteers', including officers who had 'resigned their commissions', should have made contact with the anti-Yüan southern forces at the time of the 'Second Revolution', in 1913,[34] and that a Japanese newspaper in Peking, under the protection of extraterritoriality, should openly oppose Yüan's imperial adventure.[35] Officially, several times in late 1915 and early 1916 the Japanese government, in concert with other powers and by itself, advised at least postponement. Chauvinist elements, like the *Kokuryūkai* (Amur River ['Black Dragon'] Society), resented especially what they saw as Yüan's obstructionism in the affair of the 'Twenty-one Demands', his false propaganda to curry domestic favour, his swollen 'hate Japan, love America' feeling. And spokesmen for 'East Asian principles' did not fail to indict Yüan for his breach of Confucian ethics in stabbing the Ch'ing, dishonouring his commitment, throwing in his lot with revolutionaries.[36] Such men were not disposed to let him ride with tradition. To Japanese idealists of a certain type, Yüan as strong man seemed immoral. In more matter-of-fact appraisals, he seemed inconvenient.

Yet Yüan as emperor, by his forfeiture of the support of modern-minded nationalists, actually had potentialities as China's weak man. He might have been exploitable by expansionist Japan, since he needed aid to make himself strong enough to survive, and, once surviving, to recognize his debt. Japanese support of Chinese monarchy would bring Japan at least a minority backing, minor enough to need Japan to protect its cause in China, not major enough to threaten Japan with Chinese independence. Japanese who looked on China as empty of vitality and devoid of national feeling (as many did in 1916, more than were able to later) might think this solicitude for Chinese monarchism unnecessary, and resent Yüan as an ambitious flouter of these anti-nationalist Chinese virtues.[37] But when Chinese nationalism was invoked against Yüan as emperor, invoked in its aspect of anti-traditionalism, its sanction for the free thought and open prospects which the historicism of the monarchists denied, some few Japanese discerned at last the impending maturity of Chinese nationalism. They recognized that it must work against Japan, though Japan had helped so much to bring it to birth. And they turned pro-Yüan in the end.

The famous military leader and *genro*, Yamagata, had considered the Chinese Republic, right at the start, a threat to the Japanese programme, and he fixed on Yüan as candidate for Japan's man and foe of the Republic. For Yamagata saw nationalism, bad news for Japan, in the revolution against Chinese monarchy, and anti-nationalist possibilities in Yüan's attempt to restore it. Racial solidarity, a bond between an anti-nationalist China (Emperor Yuan's?) and Japanese supporters, would define the great issues of world politics as they really were: issues of white-coloured rivalry, not of national tensions within the Asian races.[38]

The balance, nevertheless, was still against Yüan, in Japan as in China. Yet, the Hung-hsien movement was the turning point for Japan in China and Japanese influence on Chinese culture. From being the school of Chinese radicals and nationalists, Japan became the temple of the deepest Chinese traditionalism.

The Japanese 'great power' example had for a long time encouraged the Chinese new-thinkers; intellectually, Japanese had anticipated by decades the Chinese denouncers of the numbing effect of Confucian authority. In 1884, for instance, Hidaka Sanenori gave thanks that Confucianism, the binder of scholars' thoughts, had at least been confined to the East, so that science had not been stifled in the West as well. The harm brought to the world by Confucianism, he said, was much greater than the help. If only Confucianism had not been tended and developed, Eastern culture might have grown beyond the West's.[39] Even Chinese thinkers who could not go so far (like the younger K'ang Yu-wei, who would scorn most of the successors but praise Confucius himself) had looked to Japan progressive, not Japan traditionalist, as a model for China.

Yet, just when Japan, by its exertions in China, became a

target of the nationalists whom it had fostered by its example, Chinese monarchists and Confucianists, fused together by the traditionalistic spirit, turned now in their turn to a meeting with Japan, and the 'Asian' Japan, not the newly-Western, turned to seek them out. The later K'ang admired Japan as a place where men learned the *Analects* by heart in their homes, where Confucian learning was nationally respected.[40] When Yüan encouraged Confucian societies, *K'ung-chiao hui* and *Ts'un-K'ung hui*, branches appeared in Japan.[41] Under Japanese auspices, a Chinese published (in 1928!) doggedly anti-Republican references to 'the Confucian scholarship of the present dynasty'; to the 'Ju-chiao' (Confucianism) as 'the eternal standard, the indestructible principle for governing the *T'ien-hsia*'; to the state of the doubting moderns, lacking *chün* and *ch'en*, as the situation of savages.[42]

This writer went on to more of the same in 'Manchukuo' (Manchuria) during the nineteen-thirties. There the Japanese sponsored a Ch'ing revival, which drew numbers of anti-nationalists to monarchy and Confucianism. Many entered government service in the old-new dynastic state, which had *wang-tao*, the 'kingly way', as its grand Confucian pro-gramme.[43] *Wang-tao* was offered explicitly in opposition to *San min chu-i*, the Sun Yat-sen and Kuomintang 'Three People's Principles', which the Japanese and the Manchukuo men stigmatized as western.[44]

But the situation of these Chinese officials impaired the traditional wholeness of the Confucian personality. For their traditionalistic personality made them puppets, worked by the Japanese, not self-serving (in the double sense, like the old Confucian bureaucracy) in living tension with monarchy. And something else made the Confucianism of Manchukuo untraditional. What could it be but a symbol of old China, culturally 'authentic' and politically 'safe', when the sub-stance of Japanese policy there was industrial moderniza-tion?[45] Manchukuo was to feed the power of nationalist Japan with modern industry; and to sap the power of Nationalist China with an appeal to anti-modernism.

Here, then, Chinese sentiment divided, the anti-Japanese nationalist going to one of the poles and the philo-Japanese traditionalist to the other; the vestiges of monarchism were nothing more than a version of the latter. The same historical circumstances had favoured them both. Modernistic nationalism was a reaction to blows against Confucian culture, which had suffered in its central claim of universal value. And traditionalistic conservatism accepted this condition, by redefining Confucian culture as essentially Chinese, a non-universal Chinese essence. It was a dialogue of true contemporaries, no matter how premature, or how outworn, one of these Chinese parties seemed to the other.

Japan was the point of reference to which both parties turned. It was Japan, an eastern recruit to the ranks of 'western' rivals—not England, the United States or the rest—that brought home to China the contraction to China of Chinese civilization. Japan had inspired modernists in China, showing a path of resistance to the West. But when Japan itself was the sharpest spear in the Western armoury, sharper than a serpent's tooth, Chinese culture was not just hit from the outside; it was suffering defection, a significant cultural roll-back.

For the early influence of Chinese culture on Japan, where politically the Chinese nation had never really encroached, had made Chinese culture supra-national—properly, according to traditional lights. But now 'modern' Japan, no longer a vessel for Chinese influence but a vehicle for western, was only using, not living much of a Chinese traditional culture. And when in Japanese hands the culture was just a tool for a 'western' aggression, in Chinese eyes it could hardly be anything more than national. To those Chinese who compensated with nationalism for the blight on their more than national Confucian heritage, the anti-nationalist sponsorship of Confucianism only gave it a final curse. To those Chinese who felt, on the other hand, that anti-Confucianism was the curse, the national enemy was cultural friend. Paradoxically, the new Japan, which had cut Confucianism down to the organic plant that the neo-traditionalists nurtured, was the sole recourse for propping it up; though Japan, in propping it up, was taking another cut.

Thus, late monarchy, the Chinese twin of Confucianism,

was ultimately confided to foreign sponsorship. This had been foreshadowed in the ambiguous Japanese attitude toward Yüan in 1915, and it culminated in the Japanese revival of the Ch'ing dynasty in Manchuria. When nationalism implied both iconoclasm culturally and anti-Japanese feeling politically, the cause of Chinese monarchy quite plausibly qualified for Japanese backing; for with its imprisonment in cultural traditionalism, latter-day Chinese monarchy committed itself to anti-nationalism, and to a political ambiance, accordingly, at least passively pro-Japanese.

Conclusion: The Japanese and Chinese Monarchical Mystiques

IRONICALLY enough, Chinese monarchism not only ended as bankrupt with Japanese receivers, but had marked its panic long before with a desperate reaching out for Japanese procedures. The Ch'ing and their supporters, back in the days of the post-Boxer 'Manchu Reform Movement' and right down to 1911, had taken to insisting on Ch'ing eternity in the midst of the myriad changes that the Ch'ing were forced to bless, and they did it by repeating '*Wan-shih i-hsi*', the *Bansei ikkei*, 'One line throughout ten thousand ages', that celebrated Japan's imperial house.[1] It hardly belonged in China, with the latter's long centuries of non-feudal imperium, in which the mandate was not necessarily inheritable.

It is this difference between the premodern societies, Chinese bureaucratic and Japanese feudal, that accounts for the different fates of the Chinese and Japanese monarchies. In modern Japan, monarchy has been no parody, the mystique of the throne has been strengthened, not dispelled (the repercussions of the Second World War are not considered here). For in Japan, unlike China, a postfeudal régime could cite prefeudal precedents against the feudal intermission. The nineteenth-century Japanese revolution, that is, could strike against the *de facto* Tokugawa feudal shogunate (est. seventeenth century) in the name of Nara (eighth century), and Meiji (nineteenth century), *de jure* imperial control: modernization could be combined with myth-making about antiquity. But in China, the modern breach with things as they were was a breach precisely with a

136

de jure situation, a dynastic and bureaucratic régime which was, in general terms, as tradition had dictated it, and modernization required myth-breaking. Compare only the early modern contemporaries, the Chinese 'Han Learning', with its probing for forgeries and its ultimately revolutionary and republican implications, and the Japanese 'Pure Shintō', with its writing of forgeries and its ultimately revolutionary but monarchist implications. The Japanese could combine a prefeudal form with postfeudal content; the strengthening of Japanese monarchy was compatible with modernization. But the strengthening—or the mere re-establishing—of Chinese monarchy was incompatible with modernization. Indeed, as we have seen, Yüan Shih-k'ai's effort to re-establish monarchy was undertaken deliberately as an anti-modernist counterthrust.

Kokutai, or 'national form', intimately individual polity, was an ancient Japanese term with tremendous modern and nationalist-monarchist currency. But its Chinese counterpart, with the same characters, *kuo-t'i*, was just another of those terms proper to Japan, exotic in China, which were rushed to the aid of a Chinese monarchism having none of the circumstances favouring monarchy in the modern age in Japan. It was as foreign as *tsung-chiao* (religion), for example. Like the traditionalistic monarchists choosing *kokutai/kuo-t'i*, a traditionalistic Confucianist, speaking for *K'ung-chiao*, Confucianism as a religion, chose the originally Japanese compound *shūkyō* (*tsung-chiao*) to define it; indeed, he drew attention to the fact that in standard Chinese *chiao*, in such a context, stood alone.[2] As to *kuo-t'i* itself, there was no doubt about who felt most at home with it. If Chinese neo-traditionalists came to prize it, and to press it against the nationalist republicans, so did the anti-(Chinese) nationalists of Japan, following the logic of the Chinese monarchist—Japanese imperialist affinity. The well-known Japanese expansionist thinker, Kita Ikki (1882–1937), was most contemptuous of Sun Yat-sen's original American presidential model. It was bad for China, he said, because China's *kokutai* was totally different from that of the United States.[3] *Kokutai* was obviously something 'given', not a subject for experiment.

Liang Ch'i-ch'ao (1873–1929) saw the difference and the significance at the time of the Hung-hsien movement. In 1915 he rebuffed the *kuo-t'i* monarchical blandishments of Yüan's son, with their invitation to see the *kuo-ch'ing* or 'national spirit' in just this form of state. Liang preferred to speak, he said, of *cheng-t'i*, of the practical question of the workings of government rather than the more metaphysical, 'essential' question of the location of national authority[4]— this distinction having first been made as a Japanese distinction, between *kokutai* and *seitai*, in the *Kokutai Shinron* of Katō Hirayuki in 1874.[5] *Kokutai* was a living word, *kuo-t'i* was a contrivance.[6] To speak a living language, one must say that the Hung-hsien reign was supposed to be a revival of Chinese *kokutai*. But how could a Chinese *revive* in China a new and foreign importation? What was this traditional 'national form' which tradition had never named and nationalists could hardly accept? It was paradox which made of Yüan a parodist.

Yüan had hopes of Liang's support because Liang, after all, right down to 1911, had opposed the republicanism of Sun Yat-sen. Why should Liang not welcome the resumption of monarchy, and not necessarily through a Ch'ing restoration but in the time-honoured way of acknowledging change of mandate? Certainly, his defence of the Ch'ing before 1911 was more defence of monarchy (ideally, constitutional monarchy) than defence of the Manchu incumbents. He was only an anti-anti-Manchu.

And yet, confounding Yüan's hopes (both the minor one about Liang and the major one about monarchy) was the very fact, the supposedly promising fact, that Liang's support of the Ch'ing lacked any grain of positive commitment— certainly after the death in 1908 of the Kuang-hsü emperor, so sadly related to the old Reformers' cause. When Liang supported the dynasty in spite of this lack, it suggested that no dynastic succession was conceivable. And this was because the monarchical mystique was dead. If, to ward off republic and anarchy, a monarchy seemed essential, the going dynasty had to be kept going. The inertia of establishment was monarchy's only resource; if the mandate were dropped by the Ch'ing house, no Manchu, Mongol, Turk, or Chinese, whatever their fortunes in the Chinese past, would ever pick it up.

Yen Fu, more monarchist than Liang under the Republic, and in many ways a Yüan Shih-k'ai man, felt nevertheless in 1915 that Yüan was not the man of the hour, the emperor for the age. In 1917, Yen unequivocally supported the abortive restoration of the Ch'ing, all two weeks of it. He wished, though, that the circumstances of 1915 and 1917 could have been combined: Hsüan-t'ung, the last of the Ch'ing, as emperor, Yüan as prime minister.[7] What was he saying? That Yüan's talents were fine enough to make him deserve to rule. That his *mana*, his aura, was wrong. That no new claimant, however talented, could rule any longer as emperor. That only an old emperor (though in this case young in years) might conceivably sustain a precarious mass conformity, and string out the monarchical idea.

For the kings were truly finished—*wang* and *su-wang* both, the merely royal and the Confucian sage-ideal. Monarchism and Confucianism, which had belonged together in their own way and run dry together, were garbled together in a new way now that failed to elicit the old responses. When republican 'men of the future' set the pace, they not only abandoned traditionalism on their own account, but transformed the traditionalism of those who never joined them, turning it into nostalgia—which is thirst for the past, not a life-giving fluid itself.

Notes

CHAPTER I

1. *North China Herald*, CXIV, No. 2474 (Jan. 9, 1915), 87.
2. T'ao Chü-yin, *Chin-tai i-wen* (Items about the modern era) (Shanghai, 1940), 1.
3. *Faust*, Part II, Act 1, Scene 3.
4. Thomas Mann, *Doctor Faustus* (New York, 1948), 134.
5. Lu Hsün, 'Morning Flowers Gathered in the Evening', cited in Huang Sung-k'ang, *Lu Hsün and the New Culture Movement of Modern China* (Amsterdam, 1957), 40.
6. Kuzuu Yoshihisa, *Nisshi kōshō gaishi* (An unofficial history of Sino-Japanese relations) (Tokyo, 1939), 119.
7. Thurston Griggs, 'The *Ch'ing Shih Kao*: a Bibliographical Summary', *Harvard Journal of Asiatic Studies*, XVIII, Nos. 1–2 (June 1955), 115; Franklin W. Houn, *Central Government in China, 1912–1928; an Institutional Study* (Madison, 1957), 113.
8. Kao Lao, *Ti-chih yün-tung shih-mo chi* (An account of the monarchical movement) (Shanghai, 1923), 2; Yang Yu-chiung (Moriyama Takashi, tr.), *Shina Seitō shi* (History of Chinese political parties) (Tokyo, 1940), 70.
9. T'ao Chü-yin, *Pei-yang chün-fa t'ung-chih shih-ch'i shih-hua* (Historical discourses on the era of the *Pei-yang* military clique's dominion) (Peking, 1957–8), II, 28. (Hereafter, *Pei-yang chün-fa.*)
10. Kao, 17.
11. *Ibid.*, 19.
12. *Ibid.*, 18.
13. Ku Yen-wu, *Jih-chih lu* (Record of knowledge day by day), ed. Huang Ju-ch'eng (1834), 13. 5b–6a.
14. Kao, 20–21.
15. *Ibid.*, 22.
16. Chu Shou-p'eng, ed., *Kuang-hsü Tung-hua hsü-lu* (Kuang-hsü supplement to the archival records: hereafter, THL), 169, 1a.
17. e.g. THL 171. 16a; THL 184. 10a.

18. THL 199. 12b for memorialists' reference to these objectives, THL 203. 16b for edict; Imazeki Hisamaro, *Sung Yüan Ming Ch'ing Ju-chia hsüeh nien-piao* (Chronological tables of Sung, Yüan, Ming, and Ch'ing Confucianism) (Tokyo, 1920), 216 (in Chinese); Hattori Unokichi, *Kōshi oyobi Kōshikyō* (Confucius and the Confucian religion) (Tokyo, 1926), 119, 371.

19. Wu Li, 'K'ung-tzu fei Man-chou chih hu-fu' (Let Confucius not be an amulet for the Manchu), *Min-pao*, No. 11 (Jan. 30, 1907), 81.

20. Cf. Li T'ien-huai, 'Tsun K'ung shuo' (On reverence for Confucius), *Chung-kuo hsüeh-pao*, No. 7 (May 1913), 27. (Hereafter, CKHP.)

21. Kao, 7.

22. T'ao Chü-yin, *Liu chün-tzu chuan* (Biographies of the 'Six Martyrs') (Shanghai, 1946), 2. Yen's name was attached to the manifesto of the monarchist *Ch'ou-an hui* in the summer of 1915. He later maintained that this was done without his permission; though he did not disclaim it at the time (perhaps feeling this imprudent), he claimed illness as an excuse to keep out of the society's deliberations. Nevertheless, Yen was subsequently tarred with this association, which was felt to be plausible, since he had praised Yüan Shih-k'ai in 1909, when the Manchus dismissed him, and had been close to Yüan ever since the latter assumed the presidency of the Republic, offered Yen the presidency of the university in Peking, and brought him into various government offices and commissions. Cf. Yang Yin-shen, *Chung-kuo wen-hsüeh-chia lieh-chuan* (Biographies of Chinese literary figures) (Shanghai, 1939), 488–9, and Tso Shun-sheng, *Wan-chu lou sui-pi* (Sketches from the Wan-chu chamber) (Hong Kong, 1953), 36–38. Ch'en Tu-hsiu, later the first chairman of the Chinese Communist Party, flatly maintained that Yen Fu approved of Yüan's worshipping Heaven, then approved of Yüan's naming himself emperor; cf. Fukui Kōjun, *Gendai Chūgoku shisō* (Recent Chinese thought) (Tokyo, 1955), 67, 106–7. But Jerome Ch'en, *Yuan Shih-k'ai: Brutus assumes the Purple* (London, 1961), 205–6, reports that Yen Fu, hesitant, was forced to lend his name to the *Ch'ou-an hui* by pressure from Yüan, transmitted through Yang Tu, the founder of the society.

23. Chou Chen-fu, 'Yen Fu ssu-hsiang chuan pien chih p'ou-hsi' (A close analysis of the changes in Yen Fu's thought), *Hsüeh-lin*, No. 3 (Jan. 1941), 117.

24. Sakamaki Teiichirō, *Shina bunkatsu ron: tsuki, 'Gen Seikai'*

(The decomposition of China: supplement, 'Yüan Shih-k'ai') (Tokyo, 1914), 183.

25. *Ibid.*, 228, 229.

26. e.g. Rinji Taiwan kyūkan chōsakai dai-ichi-bu hōkoku (Temporary commission of the Taiwan Government-general for the study of old Chinese customs, report of the First Section), *Shinkoku gyōseihō* (Administrative laws of the Ch'ing dynasty), kan 1, revised (Tokyo, 1914), I, 46.

27. Cf. Tung Chung-shu, *Ch'un-ch'iu fan-lu* (Luxuriant dew from the Spring and Autumn Annals) (Shanghai, 1929), 10. 1b: 'The monarch who has received the mandate is given the mandate by the will of Heaven; therefore he is called the son of Heaven . . .' (This passage is also cited in Vincent Shih, *The Ideology of the T'ai-p'ing T'ien-kuo*, ms.)

28. A proper corrective to the authority cited in note 16 is Hara Tomio, *Chūka shisō no kontai to jugaku no yūi* (The roots of Chinese thought and the pre-eminence of Confucianism) (Tokyo, 1947), 183, which emphasizes that in classical Chinese thought *t'ien-i*, the will of Heaven, was independent and self-existent. That is, it was not derived from the *min-i*, the people's will, and was certainly not reduced, in the modern metaphorical fashion, to being simply a rhetorical equivalent of the latter term.

29. Sagara Yoshiaki, 'Toku no gon no igi to sono hensen' (The meaning of the word *te* and its evolution), in Tsuda Sokichi, *Tōyō shisō kenkyū* (Studies in Far Eastern thought), No. 1 (Tokyo, 1937), 290–1.

30. Wang Hsieh-chia, 'Chung-hua min-kuo hsien-fa hsüan ch'üan chang ting K'ung-chiao wei kuo-chiao ping hsü jen-min hsiu chiao tzu-yu hsiu-cheng an' (Proposal that the constitution of the Republic of China promulgate a special clause establishing Confucianism as the state religion and permitting modification of the freedom of religion), 1, 4–5, *K'ung-chiao wen-t'i* (Problems of Confucianism), No. 18, supplement (Taiyuan, 1917). (Hereafter, KCWT.)

31. *Ibid.*, 1–3.

32. Ch'ang-t'ing, 'K'ung-hsueh fa-wei' (The inner meaning of the Confucian learning revealed), CKHP, No. 1 (Nov. 1912), 4.

33. Wang Hsieh-chia, 10.

34. THL 197. 1b.

35. Sung Yü-jen, 'K'ung-hsüeh tsung-ho cheng chiao ku chin t'ung-hsi liu-pieh lun' (On Confucianism as uniter of political and intellectual, ancient and modern systems and classes), CKHP,

No. 9 (July 1913), 2; K'ang Yu-wei, 'Chung-kuo hsüeh-pao t'i-tz'u' (The thesis of the *Chung-kuo hsüeh-pao*), CKHP, No. 6 (Feb. 1913), 7, and 'Chung-kuo hsüeh-hui pao t'i-tz'u' (The thesis of the journal of the Society for Chinese Learning), *Pu-jen*, II (March 1913), *chiao-shuo*, 2.

36. Sanetō Keishū, *Nihon bunka no Shina e no eikyō* (The influence of Japanese culture on China) (Tokyo, 1940), 228; Fukui, 96.

37. 'Ta-tsung-tung kao-ling' (Presidential mandate), Sept. 25, 1914, *Chiao-yü kung-pao* (Educational record), V (June 20, 1915), *Ming-ling* 1; Nov. 3, 1914, *Chiao-yü kung-pao*, VII (Aug. 1915), *Ming-ling*, 1.

38. Henri Bernard-Maitre, *Sagesse chinoise et philosophie chrétienne* (Paris, 1935), 211; Fukui, 101–2.

39. Cf., for example, *Tsung-sheng hsüeh-pao*, the principal organ of the Confucian religionists.

40. Ch'en Huan-chang, *K'ung-chiao lun chieh-lu* (Chapters on the Confucian religion) (Taiyuan, 1918), 1b (also 7b, in the *Kung-yang*, *chin-wen* vein, for Confucius as a democrat, with the author's exculpation of Confucius's *seeming* monarchism). Ch'en, a very important editor and writer for the cause of Confucian religion, had supplemented his Chinese education with study at Columbia University and the University of Chicago. In 1912 he was one of the principal founding members of the *K'ung-chiao hui* (Confucian religious society); cf. Imazeki, 217–18.

41. Ch'en Huan-chang, 1a.

42. *Ibid.*, 2a.

43. K'ang, 'Chung-kuo hsüeh-pao t'i-tz'u', 5.

44. Tse-tsung Chow, 'The Anti-Confucian Movement in Early Republican China', *The Confucian Persuasion*, ed. Arthur F. Wright (Stanford, 1960), 297.

45. Ch'en Tu-hsiu, 'Hsien-fa yü K'ung-chiao' (The constitution and the Confucian religion), *Tu-hsiu wen-ts'un* (Collected essays of Ch'en Tu-hsiu) (Shanghai, 1937), 104–5.

46. *Ibid.*, 103.

47. Hsia Te-wo, 'Hu-nan An-hua chiao-yü-chieh ch'üan-t'i ch'ing-ting K'ung-chiao kuo-chiao shu' (Letter from the entire educational circle of An-hua, Hunan, requesting that Confucianism be established as the state religion of China), 4, KCWT, No. 17, supplement (Taiyuan, 1916).

48. Ch'en Huan-chang, 16b.

49. *Ibid.*, 16b; K'ang Yu-wei, 'K'ung-chiao hui hsü' (Preface

to the Confucian Society), *Pu-jen*, I (March 1913), *chiao-shuo* 5; K'ang Yu-wei, 'Fu Chiao-yü pu shu' (Reply to the Ministry of Education), *Pu-jen*, IV (May 1913), *chiao-shuo*, 5–6; K'ang, 'Chung-kuo hsüeh-pao t'i-tz'u', 3–4.

50. K'ang Yu-wei, 'K'ang Nan-hai chih Tsung-t'ung Tsung-li shu' (Letter from K'ang Yu-wei to the President and Premier), 2, KCWT, No. 17, supplement.

51. 'Hu-pei kung-min Liu Ta-chün shang ts'an chung liang yüan ching ting kuo-chiao shu' (Letter from Liu Ta-chün of Hupei to the parliament requesting establishment of a state religion), 4–5, KCWT, No. 18, supplement.

52. Wang Hsieh-chia, 1.

53. Hsüeh Cheng-ch'ing, 'K'ung-tzu kung-ho hsüeh-shuo' (The republican theory of Confucius), CKHP, No. 7 (May 1913) 11–12, 20, 23.

54. Li Wen-chih, 'Ching ting K'ung-chiao wei kuo-chiao ti erh-tz'u i-chien shu' (Second communication of views favouring establishment of Confucianism as the state religion), 2–3, KCWT, No. 18, supplement.

55. Liu Shih-p'ei, 'Chün-cheng fu-ku lun (chung)' (On the monarchical revival, part two), CKHP, No. 2 (Feb. 1916), 3.

56. Fukui, 1, for this response, in the seventeenth century, to Jesuit reports of the founding of the Dutch Republic.

57. K'ang, 'Chung-kuo hsüeh-pao t'i-tz'u', 13.

58. Cf. D. W. Brogan, 'The "Nouvelle Revue Française" ', *Encounter* (March 1959), 66: ' . . . this is a French inspection of the French mind almost as introverted as if it had been produced around 1680. . . . But France in 1680, in most realms of thought and action, was dominant in Europe. France in the heyday of the NRF was not. Necessarily, a nation-centred culture in a nation that is no longer the centre of a super-national culture must be parochial. . . .'

CHAPTER II

1. For example, cf. Jacques Gernet, *Les aspects économiques du Bouddhisme dans la société chinoise du Ve au Xe siècle* (Saigon, 1956), 293–4 et seq., for the exploitation of Buddhism to support the imperial power. To cite a later period: Ming imperial indulgence toward Buddhism was marked. Even while Confucian scholars biased in favour of their master, the Yung-lo emperor (reigned 1403–24), taxed his predecessor (whose throne he had usurped)

with favour to Buddhists, Yung-lo himself retained his ties with the monks who had helped him to power; see Chapter III.

2. For the Buddhist contribution to trade and capital formation, see Gernet, esp. 138–90.

3. J. J. L. Duyvendak, *China's Discovery of Africa* (London, 1949), 27–28.

4. For Ming, see Charles Whitman MacSherry, 'Impairment of the Ming Tributary System as Exhibited in Trade Involving Fukien', unpublished Ph.D. dissertation, University of California, 1957.

5. For the Hoppo's appointment by the 'inner court' (imperial) rather than the 'outer court' (general bureaucratic), see William Frederick Mayers, *The Chinese Government* (Shanghai, 1886), 40; and for his practice of sending memorials directly to the emperor, not through normal channels, see *Shinkoku gyōseihō*, kan 5 (Tokyo, 1911), 311–12.

6. See the chapter, 'The Amateur Ideal in Ming and Early Ch'ing Society: Evidence from Painting', in Volume One of this work, 15–43. It is interesting to note that a Chinese Communist critic, in the interests of isolating the literati tradition as 'the enemy', has set the 'academic' style apart (the Sung Emperor Hui-tsung is specifically praised) as the anti-Confucian precedent for the Communist-sponsored 'realism' in art; see Chang Jen-hsia, 'Flower-and-Bird Painting', *China Reconstructs*, III (May–June 1953), 51.

7. Cf. Joseph R. Strayer, 'Feudalism in Western Europe', *Feudalism in History*, ed. Rushton Coulborn (Princeton, 1956), 23.

8. Pan Ku, *The History of the Former Han Dynasty*, tr. Homer H. Dubs, Vol. Two (Baltimore, 1944), 292. As Pow-key Sohn has pointed out in 'The Theory and Practice of Land-systems in Korea in Comparison with China' (ms. University of California, 1956), the Koryö victory of military over civil interests played a large part in defeating the trend in Korea toward a private-property system; it encouraged, rather, a return to a strict system of state ownership and state allocation—a system, be it noted, which T'ang and other rulers in China favoured at times, but which civil-official recalcitrance broke down.

9. Tezuka Ryōdō, *Jukyō dōtoku ni okeru kunshin shisō* (The sovereign-minister idea in Confucian ethics) (Tokyo, 1925), 112; Miyakawa Hisayuki, 'Zenjō ni yoru ōchō kakumei no tokushitsu' (The special quality of dynastic overturns depending on '*shan-jang*'), *Tōhōgaku*, No. 11 (Oct. 1955), 50.

10. *Ming-shih*, Shih-huo chih, ch. 77, 11a–11b, cited in Shih ms.

11. As Shih points out, the Taiping state stressed the motto, *i hsiao tso chung*, 'transform filial piety into loyalty'. The Taipings seem to me to represent in Chinese history (among other things) the assertion of a pure monarchical spirit, i.e. a spirit of un-qualified autocracy, a refusal to compromise with bureaucratic ideals. A régime which understandably alienated the Confucian literati unequivocally, the Taiping state was trying to rule out the possibility of the traditional intra-bureaucratic conflict between private and public impulses.

12. Carsun Chang, *The Development of Neo-Confucian Thought* (New York, 1957), 203.

13. See R. H. van Gulik, tr., *T'ang-Yun-Pi-Shih, 'Parallel Cases from under the Pear-Tree'* (Leiden, 1956), vii, for the oft-quoted statement applying to the scholar-official, 'One does not read the Code', and its bearing on theories of the ideal state and ideal ruler.

14. Louis Delatte, *Les traités de la royauté d'Ecphante, Diotegène, et Sthénidas* (Liege and Paris, 1942), 140–2.

15. Shōji Sōichi, 'Chin Ryō no gaku' (The thought of Ch'en Liang), *Tōyō no bunka to shakai*, IV (1954), 98–100.

16. Cf. J. Walter Jones, *The Law and Legal Theory of the Greeks* (Oxford, 1956), 292–3.

CHAPTER III

1. For the monarchical interest in 'field-limitation' or 'field-equalization' (*hsien-t'ien, chün-t'ien*), see Joseph R. Levenson, 'Ill Wind in the Well-field: the Erosion of the Confucian Ground of Controversy', *The Confucian Persuasion*, ed. Arthur F. Wright (Stanford, 1960), 268–87; and Volume Three.

2. Niida Noboru, *Chūgoku no nōson kazoku* (The Chinese peasant family) (Tokyo, 1952), 105–6.

3. C. H. Brewitt-Taylor, tr., *The Romance of the Three Kingdoms* (Shanghai, 1925), I, 581–2.

4. Shimizu Morimitsu, 'Kyū Shina ni okeru sensei kenryoku no kiso' (The basis of autocratic power in pre-revolutionary China), *Mantetsu chōsa geppō* (Bulletin of the research bureau of the South Manchuria Railway), XVII, No. 2 (Feb. 1937), 9.

5. Liang Ch'i-ch'ao, 'Chung-kuo chih wu-shih-tao' (China's *bushidō*), *Yin-ping-shih ho-chi* (Shanghai, 1936), *ch'uan-chi* 6: 24. 60–61.

6. Ch'ien Mu, *Kuo-shih ta-kang* (Outline of Chinese history) (Shanghai, 1940), I, 354. For a summary of literature on the examination system, matured by Sung, as an enhancer of monarchical absolutism over aristocratic privilege, see Wolfgang Franke, *The Reform and Abolition of the Traditional Chinese Examination System* (Cambridge, Mass., 1960), 2–7.

7. Max Weber, 'Politics as a Vocation', *From Max Weber: Essays in Sociology*, ed. H. H. Gerth and C. Wright Mills (New York, 1946), 78, 82.

8. Montesquieu, *The Spirit of the Laws*, tr. Thomas Nugent (New York, 1949), I, 16.

9. For a similar analysis and an application of it, see L. A. Fallers, 'Despotism, Status Culture and Social Mobility in an African Kingdom', *Comparative Studies in Society and History*, II, No. 1 (Oct. 1959), 11–32.

10. George Orwell, *The English People* (London, 1947), 25.

11. Leonard Krieger, *The German Idea of Freedom: History of a Political Tradition* (Boston, 1957), 16–17.

12. Andrew Alföldi, *A Conflict of Ideas in the Late Roman Empire: the Clash between the Senate and Valentinian I* (Oxford, 1952), 51–57.

13. William G. Sinnigen, 'The Vicarius Urbis Romae and the Urban Prefecture', *Historia*, VIII, No. 1 (Jan. 1959), 112; William Gurnee Sinnigen, *The Officium of the Urban Prefecture During the Later Roman Empire* (Rome, 1957), 5.

14. Ernst Kantorowicz, *Frederick the Second (1194–1250)* (London, 1931), 227–38, 519.

15. Robert Lee Wolff, 'The Three Romes: the Migration of an Ideology and the Making of an Autocrat', *Daedalus* (Spring 1959), 302–3; George Vernadsky, *A History of Russia* (New Haven, 1951), 66–68, 78.

16. G. d'Avenel, *La noblesse française sous Richelieu* (Paris, 1901), 342; Franklin T. Ford, *Robe and Sword: the Regrouping of the French Aristocracy after Louis XIV* (Cambridge, Mass., 1953), 6–7.

17. Alexis de Tocqueville, *The Old Régime and the French Revolution* (New York, 1955), 26–28, 58; Hippolyte Adolphe Taine, *The Ancient Régime* (New York, 1931), I, 36–37, 43–44; Elinor G. Barber, *The Bourgeoisie in 18th Century France* (Princeton, 1955), 128. Lucy Norton, tr., *Saint-Simon at Versailles* (New York, 1958).

18. d'Avenel, 11.

19. Georges Lefebvre, *The Coming of the French Revolution, 1789* (Princeton, 1947), 16; Alfred Cobban, *A History of Modern France:*

I, Old Régime and Revolution, 1715–1799 (Harmondsworth, 1957), 20–21.

20. Franz Neumann, 'Montesquieu', *The Democratic and Authoritarian State: Essays in Political and Legal Theory* (Glencoe, 1957), 106; Peter Gay, *Voltaire's Politics: the Poet as Realist* (Princeton, 1959), 90–91.

21. Wolfgang H. Kraus, 'Authority, Progress, and Colonialism', *Nomos I: Authority,* ed. Carl J. Friedrich (Cambridge, 1958), 148; Hans Rosenberg, *Bureaucracy, Aristocracy, and Autocracy: the Prussian Experience, 1660–1815* (Cambridge, 1958), 43–75; Otto Hintze, 'Staatsverfassung und Heeresverfassung', *Staat und Verfassung: Gesammelte Abhandlungen zur Allgemeinen Verfassungsgeschichte* (Leipzig, 1941), 61–62.

22. Lü Ssu-mien, *Chung-kuo t'ung-shih* (General History of China) (n.p., 1941), II, 390.

23. *Ibid.,* II, 397.

24. Edwin G. Pulleyblank, *The Background of the Rebellion of An Lu-shan* (London, New York, and Toronto, 1955), 47–48.

25. Miyazaki Ichisada, *Yō-sei-tei, Chugoku no dokusai kunshu* (The Yung-cheng Emperor—China's autocratic ruler) (Tokyo, 1950), 24.

26. Cf. Jacques Gernet, *Daily Life in China on the Eve of the Mongol Invasion, 1250–1276* (New York, 1962), 75.

27. David B. Chan, 'The Problem of the Princes As Faced by the Ming Emperor Hui (1399–1402)', *Oriens,* XI, No. 1–2 (1958), 184–5; C. T. Hu, 'The Ning Wang Revolt: Sociology of a Ming Rebellion', ms. read at annual meeting of Association for Asian Studies, 1959.

28. *Shinkoku gyōseihō,* kan 1, I, 119.

29. *Ibid.,* I, 122.

30. Cf. reference to the Hsiang K'ai memorial of A.D. 166 in E. Zürcher, *The Buddhist Conquest of China: the Spread and Adaptation of Buddhism in Early Medieval China* (Leiden, 1959), I, 37.

31. Howard S. Levy, *Biography of Huang Ch'ao* (Berkeley and Los Angeles, 1955), 54.

32. Naitō Torajiro, *Shinchō shi tsūron* (Outline of Ch'ing history) (Tokyo, 1944), 31–32.

33. Taine, I, 37, 43–44.

34. Rosenberg, 139, 151–2, 186–8, 201.

35. W. H. Bruford, 'The Idea of "Bildung" in Wilhelm von Humboldt's Letters', *The Era of Goethe: Essays Presented to James Boyd* (Oxford, 1959), 21, 32, 34, 38, 45.

36. Cf. Fritz Morstein Marx, *The Administrative State: an Introduction to Bureaucracy* (Chicago, 1957), 164.

37. Chao Yuen Ren, 'What is Correct Chinese?', *Journal of the American Oriental Society*, LXXXI, No. 3 (Aug.–Sept. 1961), 171–2.

38. David B. Chan, 'The Role of the Monk Tao-Yen in the Usurpation of the Prince of Yen (1398–1402)', *Sinologica*, VI, No. 2 (1959), 95–96.

CHAPTER IV

1. Benjamin Schwartz, 'Some Polarities in Confucian Thought', *Confucianism in Action*, ed. David S. Nivison and Arthur F. Wright (Stanford, 1959), 50–63.

2. Burton Watson, *Ssu-ma Ch'ien. Grand Historian of China* (New York, 1958), 173–4.

3. Chang Hsüeh-ch'eng (1738–1801), recognizing the vagaries of *shih*, the times, for the realization of sage-wisdom in action; quoted in Nomura Kōichi, 'Seimatsu Kōyō gakuha no keisei to Kō Yūi gaku no rekishiteki igi' (The formation of the late-Ch'ing *kung-yang* school, and the historical meaning of K'ang Yu-wei's doctrine), Part I, *Kokka gakkai zasshi*, LXXI, No. 7 (1958), 22.

4. Frederick Mote, 'Confucian Eremitism in the Yuan Period', *The Confucian Persuasion*, 225.

5. W. Theodore de Bary, 'A Reappraisal of Neo-Confucianism', *Studies in Chinese Thought*, ed. Arthur F. Wright (Chicago, 1953), 86–87.

6. See above, Chapter II, for Chu Hsi vs. Ch'en Liang, with another version of the *hsiu-shen p'ing t'ien-hsia* polarity.

7. For Chu Hsi on Fan Chung-yen, see James T. C. Liu, 'Some Classifications of Bureaucrats in Chinese Historiography', *Confucianism in Action*, 173. For Fan on clan properties, as discussed below, see Denis Twitchett, 'The Fan Clan's Charitable Estates, 1050–1710', *ibid.*, 100–8.

8. See Hui-chen Wang Liu, 'An Analysis of Chinese Clan Rules: Confucian Theories in Action', *ibid.*, 72–77.

9. For the State's ambivalent indulgence and restraint of clans, see *ibid.*, 75–76, for eighteenth-century examples; and Maurice Freedman, 'The Family in China, Past and Present', *Pacific Affairs*, XXXIV, No. 4 (Winter 1961–2), 325.

10. For the ambiguity of the gentry's position between clan and state, and the clan and secret society as rival alignments based

on different conceptions of kinship, see Maurice Freedman, *Lineage Organization in Southeastern China* (London, 1958), 123–5.

11. Araki Toshikazu, 'Sō-dai okeru denshi seiritsu no jijō' (Circumstances leading to the establishment of the palace examinations), *Tō-A jimbun gakuhō*, III, No. 2 (Oct. 1943), 223–4.

12. Miyazaki, 96–97.

13. Arthur Waley, *Yuan Mei, Eighteenth Century Chinese Poet* (New York, 1956), 57; and (following Waley) Robert M. Marsh, 'Bureaucratic Constraints on Nepotism in the Ch'ing Period', *Journal of Asian Studies*, XIX, No. 2 (Feb. 1960), 121.

14. Marsh, 126.

15. Ping-ti Ho, 'Aspects of Social Mobility in China, 1368–1911', *Comparative Studies in Society and History*, I, No. 4 (June 1959), 345.

16. See E. G. Pulleyblank, 'Neo-Confucianism and Neo-Legalism in T'ang Intellectual Life, 755–805', *The Confucian Persuasion*, 93.

17. In *The Confucian Persuasion*.

18. 'The Amateur Ideal in Ming and Early Ch'ing China: Evidence from Painting', *Chinese Thought and Institutions*, ed. John K. Fairbank (Chicago, 1957), 325–34; and *Confucian China and its Modern Fate*, I, 22–34.

19. Cf. James F. Cahill, 'Confucian Elements in the Theory of Painting', *The Confucian Persuasion*, 115–40.

20. Moses Hadas, *Hellenistic Culture: Fusion and Diffusion* (New York, 1959), 68.

21. Alexander Soper, 'Standards of Quality in Northern Sung Painting', *Archives of the Chinese Art Society of America*, XI (1957), 9.

22. A seventeenth-century quotation from an earlier work; cited in Franke, 22.

23. Karl A. Wittfogel and Feng Chia-sheng, *History of Chinese Society: Liao (907–1125)* (Philadelphia, 1949), 456–63.

24. Alföldi, 51.

25. Kung-chuan Hsiao, *Rural China: Imperial Control in the Nineteenth Century* (Seattle, 1960), 4, 8.

CHAPTER V

1. See Arthur F. Wright, 'Sui Yang-ti: Personality and Stereotype', *The Confucian Persuasion*, 47–49, 59–65.

2. See Mote, 208, 220, 229–40.

3. Joshua Liao, 'The Empire Breaker', *The Orient*, 10 (May 1951), 27.

4. Charles O. Hucker, 'Confucianism and the Chinese Censorial System', *Confucianism in Action*, 208.

5. Ch'en Yin-k'o, *T'ang-tai cheng-shih shih shu-lun kao* (Draft account of T'ang political history) (Shanghai, 1947), 26—quoting a thirteenth-century commentary on the *Tzu-chih t'ung-chien* of Ssu-ma Kuang.

6. See Volume One, Chapter II.

7. So defined in Karl A. Wittfogel, *Oriental Despotism: A Comparative Study of Total Power* (New Haven, 1957), 153.

8. Leon Hurvitz, ' "Render unto Caesar" in Early Chinese Buddhism', *Sino-Indian Studies: Liebenthal Festschrift*, ed. Kshitis Roy (Visvabharati, 1957), 81.

9. Mark Mancall, 'China's First Missions to Russia, 1729–1731', *Papers on China*, IX (Harvard University, August 1955), 87, 99, Mancall, 102, makes several conjectures as to why a Chinese record of the episode is not extant. Any one of these is plausible, but they do not extend to the possibility of different Confucian and imperial conceptions of kingship.

10. *The Dawn*, cited in Walter Kaufmann, *Nietzsche* (New York, 1956), 164.

11. David S. Nivison, 'Ho-shen and His Accusers: Ideology and Political Behavior in the Eighteenth Century', *Confucianism in Action*, 227. See also Marsh, 131–2, for the imperially sponsored central-bureaucratic demand that Ch'ing officials' obligations to the throne take precedence over the Confucian-prescribed bonds of family and friendship.

12. Miyazaki, 76–80.

13. Ping-ti Ho, *Studies on the Population of China, 1368–1953* (Cambridge, Mass., 1959), 215.

14. Miyazaki, 92.

15. Nivison, 'Ho Shen and His Accusers', 231.

16. Levenson, 'Ill Wind in the Well-field', 270–1, see also Vol. III.

17. Ch'en Po-ying, *Chung-kuo t'ien-chih ts'ung-k'ao* (General survey of Chinese land systems) (Shanghai, 1935), 240.

18. Miyazaki, 97.

19. W. T. de Bary, 'Chinese Despotism and the Confucian Ideal: a Seventeenth-Century View', *Chinese Thought and Institutions*, 171; Joseph R. Levenson, *Confucian China and Its Modern Fate*, I, 100–1.

20. Shimizu, 13.
21. *Shinkoku gyōseihō*, kan 1, I, 48, 139–41. Lien-sheng Yang, 'Notes on Dr. Swann's "Food and Money in Ancient China" ', *Studies in Chinese Institutional History* (Cambridge, Mass., 1961), 89–90, discusses the at least nominal distinction under most of the major dynasties, dating back to Han, between the emperor's purse and the empire's purse. Nineteenth-century Ch'ing officials, among others, remonstrated against the imperial penchant for confounding the two.

CHAPTER VI

1. Robert des Rotours, *La traité des examens, traduit de la Nouvelle Histoire des T'ang* (Paris, 1932), 172–3.
2. *Shinkoku gyōseihō*, kan 4 (Tokyo, 1911), 82, 89.
3. *Ibid.*, 93–106.
4. Norman Cohn, *The Pursuit of the Millennium* (London, 1957), 216.
5. George Rude, *The Crowd in the French Revolution* (Oxford, 1959), 227.
6. de Tocqueville, 8.
7. *Ibid.*, 8.
8. E.g. Tocqueville's ancestor Lamoignon de Malesherbes; cf. Richard Herr, *Tocqueville and the Old Régime* (Princeton, 1962), 88.
9. Georges Lefebvre, *Etudes sur la Revolution française* (Paris, 1954), 322–3; Lefebvre, *The Coming of the French Revolution, 1789*, 3.
10. For the growing hatred of aristocrats as anachronisms, beneficiaries bereft of the functions which once had been their justification, and for the king's involvement, see de Tocqueville, 30; Taine, I, 26, 36, 40, 43–44, 77–80, 85; Cobban, 108, 253; and Joseph Schumpeter, 'The Sociology of Imperialism', *'Imperialism' and 'Social Classes'* (New York, 1955), 57–58. Ford, 201, 251, points out that the 'robe' nobility of the *parlements*, the nearest thing left, after Louis XIV's domination of the aristocracy, to an aristocracy of function (and accordingly subject to seventeenth-century 'sword' contempt as upstarts from beyond the ranks of the nobility of 'courage'), became more and more functionless, and leaders in the common defence of privilege.
11. Lefebvre, *The Coming of the French Revolution, 1789*, 17; Barber, 102; R. R. Palmer, 'Georges Lefebvre: The Peasants and

the French Revolution', *Journal of Modern History*, XXXI, No. 4 (Dec. 1959), 339.

12. Herr, 120; Gay, 8; Douglas Dakin, *Turgot and the Ancient Régime in France* (London, 1939), 27–31.

13. Lefebvre, *The Coming of the French Revolution, 1789*, 61.

14. Barber, 136; d'Avenel, 286–7.

15. Gabriel Hanotaux and Le Duc de la Force, *Histoire du Cardinal de Richelieu* (Paris, 1899), VI, 306, 322.

16. Gay, 318.

17. See d'Avenel, 282–6, for a description of the ignorance to be found among aristocrats in Richelieu's day, while the intellectual world was attracting *bourgeois*.

18. Denis Diderot, 'The Encyclopaedia', '*Rameau's Nephew*', *and other Works*, tr. Jacques Barzun and Ralph H. Bowen (New York, 1956), 301–2.

19. Nomura, 9–13.

20. Wei Yüan, *Ku-wei t'ang chi*, 1878 (Huai-nan shu-chü ed.), ch. 2. 22b–23a.

CHAPTER VII

1. Eugene Powers Boardman, *Christian Influence Upon the Ideology of the Taiping Rebellion, 1851–1864* (Madison, 1952), 124–5.

2. Henri Maspéro, *Etudes historiques* (Paris, 1950), 214–15.

3. According to Tung Chung-shu (second century B.C.), Confucius received the 'Imperial Mandate' in principle; see Fung Yu-lan, *A History of Chinese Philosophy*, Vol. II (Princeton, 1953), 63, 71, 129. For Confucius as *su-wang* see Tu Yü (222–84), *Ch'un-ch'iu Tso-chuan hsü* (Preface to *Ch'un-ch'iu*, with *Tso-chuan*): cf. *Tz'u-hai*, II, 61.

4. The 'Norman Anonymous' of York (*c.* 1100), in Ernst H. Kantorowicz, *The King's Two Bodies: a Study in Mediaeval Political Theology* (Princeton, 1957), 47–48, 63.

5. Ernst H. Kantorowicz, *Laudes Regiae: a Study in Liturgical Acclamations and Mediaeval Ruler Worship* (Berkeley and Los Angeles, 1946), 13–31.

6. Medieval Russian chronicle, continuing a Byzantine tradition of the sanctity of power, quoted in Michael Cherniavsky, *Tsar and People: Studies in Russian Myths* (New Haven and London, 1961), 12.

7. Tu Ehr-wei, *Chung-kuo ku-tai tsung-chiao yen-chiu* (Studies on the ancient religions of China) (Taipei, 1959), 84–88, 106–10.

8. A. Marmorstein, *The Old Rabbinic Doctrine of God* (London, 1927), I, 105–7.

9. Toda Toyosaburō, 'Gogyō setsu seiritsu no ichi kōsatsu' (Reflection on the formation of five-element theory), *Shinagaku kenkyū*, XII (1956), 44.

10. Hattori, 231.

11. Fung Yu-lan, *A History of Chinese Philosophy*, Vol. I (Peiping, 1937), 162–3.

12. Salo Wittmayer Baron, *A Social and Religious History of the Jews* (New York, 1952), I, Chapter One (esp. 4–8); E. I. J. Rosenthal, 'Some Aspects of the Hebrew Monarchy', *The Journal of Jewish Studies*, IX, Nos. 1 and 2 (1958), 18.

13. Hara, 233.

14. Ch'eng Hao, 'Lun wang pa cha-tzu' (Memorial on *wang* and *pa*), *Erh Ch'eng wen-chi* (Collection of writings of the two Ch'engs) (Changsha, 1941), 4.

15. Waley, 54–55.

16. Ewart Lewis, *Medieval Political Ideas* (New York, 1954), I, 142–3.

17. Moses Maimonides, *Guide of the Perplexed*, tr. M. Friedländer (New York, n.d.), II, 190.

18. Yang Yu-chiung, *Chung-kuo cheng-chih ssu-hsiang shih* (History of Chinese Political Thought) (Shanghai, 1937), 181–3; Tung Chung-shu, 19b.

19. Kantorowicz, *The King's Two Bodies*, 61–78, 87–93 et passim; *Laudes Regiae*, 145–6.

20. Hugh of Fleury, 'Tractatus de Regia Potestate et Sacerdotali', (*c.* 1102), quoted in Lewis, I, 166–8.

21. Marc Bloch, *Les rois thaumaturges* (Strasbourg, 1924), 20, 140–4, 215.

22. J. W. N. Watkins, 'Milton's Vision of a Reformed England', *The Listener*, LXI, No. 1556 (Jan. 22, 1959), 169.

23. Guglielmo Ferrero, *The Principles of Power* (New York, 1942), 150, observes that when Moses here prescribed that the king 'shall not multiply horses to himself', and that 'neither shall he greatly multiply to himself silver and gold', he condemned monarchy as the West has conceived it since the Middle Ages.

24. Ford, 9. This is precisely the materialist interpretation of the origins of Biblical monotheism in M. J. Shakhnovich, *Reaktsionnaia sushchnost' Iudaizma: Kratkii ocherk proiokhozhdeniia i*

klas-sovoi sushchnosti iudeskoi religii (The reactionary essence of Judaism: a short sketch of the derivation and class nature of the Jewish religion) (Moscow, Leningrad, 1960). See review in *Judaism*, XI, No. 1 (Winter 1962), 74.

25. Harry Austryn Wolfson, *Philo: Foundations of Religious Philosophy in Judaism, Christianity and Islam* (Cambridge, Mass., 1947), II, 331, 334–7, 381–2.

26. Michael Grant, *From Imperium to Auctoritas: a Historical Study of Aes Coinage in the Roman Empire, 49 B.C.–A.D. 14* (Cambridge, 1946), 356–9.

27. Erwin I. J. Rosenthal, *Political Thought in Mediaeval Islam: an Introductory Outline* (Cambridge, 1958), 43, 219.

28. Zevedei Barbu, *Problems of Historical Psychology* (New York, 1960), 68; Lucien Febvre, *Au coeur religieux du XVIᵉ siècle* (Paris, 1957), 264–5.

29. Norman H. Baynes, *Byzantine Studies and Other Essays* (London, 1955), 55–57.

30. *Ibid.*, 168.

31. The *su-wang*, as the true sage and an implied rebuke to the politically visible royal incumbent, figures in the Taoist *Chuang-tzu* (T'ien-tao section); see Tz'u-hai, II, 61; also Inoue Gengo, 'Juka to Haku I Tō Seki setsuwa' (Confucianism and the tales of Po I and Tao Chih), *Shinagaku kenkyū*, No. 13 (Sept. 1955), 21, where *Kung-yang* Confucian influence on Chuang-tzu is seen in the *su-wang* concept. In so far as we speak of Taoism as politically anarchistic, we identify it with an *essential* Confucianism which affects Confucianism-in-action, but is not coterminous with it. The Confucianism which is implemented, visible in history, is the credo of officials, who are naturally no anarchists. But the Taoist boycott of the world of affairs (as by hermits, who flout the values of Confucian-in-action, i.e. Confucianism-cum-Legalism, but confirm them, too, by abandoning the world to Confucianists—and dynasts—alone) dramatizes the theoretical principle which Confucianists invoke, as Confucianism-cum-Taoism, to rebuke emperors.

32. Cf. Howard S. Levy, tr., *Biography of An Lu-shan* (Berkeley and Los Angeles, 1960), 19, for a *Chiu T'ang-shu* indictment of the rebellion-cursed eighth-century Emperor Hsüan-tsung as a believer in the Taoist doctrine of *wu-wei*, inactivity.

33. Cf. Manegold of Lautenbach (a partisan of the greatest anti-imperial pope, Gregory VII), 'Ad Gebehardum Liber' (*c.* 1085), quoted in Lewis, I, 165: 'Therefore it is necessary that

he who is to bear the charge of all and govern all should shine above others in greatest grace of the virtues. . . . Yet when he who has been chosen for the coercion of the wicked and the defence of the upright has begun to foster evil against them . . . is it not clear that he deservedly falls from the dignity entrusted to him and that the people stand free of his lordship and subjection . . .?'

CHAPTER VIII

1. Wolff, 304.
2. A rebel proclamation addressed to the Ch'ing emperor in 1853 assailed the latter's ancestors for betrayal of the 'good government of the Ming' in 1644, and referred to the rebel claimant as the seventh descendant of the Ming Emperor Kuang-tsung (1620–1). See 'T'ien-ti hui chao-shu' (Decree of the *T'ien-ti hui*), *T'ai-p'ing T'ien-kuo shih-liao* (Historical materials on the *T'ai-p'ing T'ien-kuo*), ed. Chin Yü-fu et al. (Peking, 1955) (hereafter TPTKSL), 256; 'Passing Events in China (from Dr. D. J. MacGowan's Note Book)', *North China Herald* (hereafter NCH), No. 159 (Aug. 13, 1853), 7.
3. See *T'ai-ping T'ien-kuo* (The Heavenly Kingdom of Great Peace), ed. Hsiang Ta et al (Shanghai, 1952) (hereafter TPTK), I, frontispiece and caption. *The North China Herald* originally gave the impression that T'ien-te and Hung were the same person: e.g. in 'Proclamation of One of the Insurgent Chiefs', NCH No. 137 (March 12, 1853), 126. But later in the year a correspondent noted that, after the recent fall of Nanking to the Taipings, no more T'ien-te proclamations had been issued, and the Taipings were said to deny his existence. The correspondent conjectured the existence of two parties, one of Ming legitimists, who spoke in the name of T'ien-te or Huang-ti, and the other of Taiping rebels, who considered the use of *ti* in a sovereign's designation as blasphemous, since they reserved it for God. See 'Passing Events in China', 7.

The personal name of T'ien-te was Hung Ta-ch'üan. In Ch'ing official sources, he was identified as T'ien-te and taken to be Taiping co-sovereign with Hung Hsiu-ch'üan; see Teng Ssu-yü, 'Hung Hsiu-ch'üan', in Arthur W. Hummel, ed. *Eminent Chinese of the Ch'ing Period* (Washington, 1943), I, 363. For Hung Ta-ch'üan correctly identified as T'ien-te Wang in the ranks of the *T'ien-ti hui*, see Kuo Ting-yee, *T'ai-p'ing T'ien-kuo shih jih-chih*

(Daily record of *T'ai-p'ing T'ien-kuo* historical events) (Shanghai, 1946), II, Appendix, 37.

4. 'Hsü Chien-chieh kao-shih' (Proclamation by Hsü Chien-chieh), TPTK, II, 893.

5. 'Hsün-t'ien Huang-ti chao' (Proclamation of the Hsün-t'ien Emperor), TPTKSL, 255; 'T'ien-te Wang t'ieh Liu-chou kao-shih' (Proclamation of T'ien-te Wang affixed at Liu-chou), TPTK, II, 891; 'T'ien-ti hui chao-shu', 256, and 'Passing Events in China', 7; 'Proclamation of One of the Insurgent Chiefs', 126.

6. 'Huang Wei kao-shih' (Proclamation by Huang Wei), TPTK, II, 898.

7. Ku Yen-wu, *Jih-chih lu* (Record of knowledge day by day) (Jui-ch'u t'ang ed., 1695), ch. 4.8a.

8. 'Ch'in-ting shih-chiai t'iao-li' (By imperial order: regulations for official ranks), TPTK, II, 551.

9. 'Pien yao-hsüeh wei tsui-li lun' (Despising the pit of fiends as durance vile), TPTK, I, 293.

10. Yang Yu-ch'iung, 181.

11. 'Chien T'ien-ching yü Chin-liang lun' (On building the Heavenly Capital in Nanking), TPTK, I, 267, 269.

12. 'T'ien-ming chao-chih-shu' (Book of heavenly decrees and imperial edicts), TPTK, I, 59–61; 'The Book of Celestial Decrees and Declarations of the Imperial Will', NCH, No. 148 (May 28, 1853), 172.

13. See *Lun-yü*, 'The Analects', XVII, 2–3: 'The Master said, "I would prefer not speaking." Tsze-kung said, "If you, Master, do not speak, what shall we, your disciples, have to record?" The Master said, "Does Heaven speak? The four seasons pursue their courses and all things are *continually* being produced, *but* does Heaven say anything?" ' Cf. 'T'ien-fu hsia-fan chao-shu' (Book of declarations of the divine will made during the Heavenly Father's descent upon earth), TPTK, I, 9 (NCH, No. 149 (June 4, 1853), 175), where *T'ien-fu* speaks to *T'ien-wang*.

14. 'Chao-shu kai-nien pan-hsing lun' (On the promulgation of imperial proclamations under fixed seal), TPTK, I, 313.

15. Cf. 'Chen T'ien-ming T'ai-p'ing T'ien-kuo . . .' in Yang Hsiu-ch'ing Hsiao Ch'ao-kuei hui-hsien kao-yü (Joint proclamation of Yang Hsiu-ch'ing and Hsiao Ch'ao-kuei), TPTK, II, 691; NCH, No. 151 (June 18, 1853), 182.

16. 'T'ien-fu hsia-fan chao-shu', 10; NCH, No. 149, 175.

17. 'T'ien-lu yao-lun' (On the essentials of the principles of Heaven), TPTK, I, 345–8 et passim; 'T'ien-t'iao shu' (Book of the

¹aws of Heaven), TPTK, I, 73 ('The Book of Religious Precepts of the T'hae-ping Dynasty', NCH, No. 146 [May 14, 1853], 163). The NCH article corresponds to 'T'ien-t'iao shu' only in certain passages.

18. 'T'ien-ming chao-chih-shu', 67; NCH, No. 148, 172.

19. 'T'ai-p'ing chiu-shih-ko' (Taiping songs on salvation), TPTK, I, 242–3; NCH, No. 178 (Dec. 24, 1853), 83.

20. 'Ch'in-ting ying-chieh kuei-chen' (By imperial order: a hero returning to truth), TPTK, II, 574–5.

21. 'Ch'in-ting shih-chiai t'iao-li' (By imperial order: regulations for official ranks), TPTK, II, 546, 552, 561.

22. 'Tsei-ch'ing hui-tsuan' (Collected materials on the circumstances of the thieves), TPTK, III, 112.

23. 'T'ai-p'ing T'ien-jih' (Taiping days), TPTK, II, 635–6.

24. 'Pan-hsing chao-shu' (Proclamations published by imperial authority), TPTK, I, 164.

25. 'T'ien-t'iao shu', 74.

26. 'Chien T'ien-ching yü Chin-ling lun', 261.

27. 'T'ien-t'iao shu', 73. See NCH, No. 146 (May 14, 1853), 163, for a translation of another version of this sentiment.

28. Boardman, 116, following Chien Yu-wen.

29. 'T'ien-ch'ing tao-li shu' (Book of the divine nature and principles), TPTK, I, 360.

30. See Boardman, 4, for the Western denunciation of this claim as blasphemy.

31. 'T'ai-p'ing chao-shu' (Taiping imperial proclamations), TPTK, I, 92; NCH, No. 150 (June 11, 1853), 180; James Legge, *the Li Ki*, Books I–X, *Sacred Books of the East*, ed. F. Max Müller (Oxford, 1885), 364.

32. 'T'ai-p'ing chao-shu', 88; NCH, Nos. 150–80. It should be noted in this connection that the Taipings held that God could be worshipped by all the people, not just by sovereign princes, in marked contradistinction to the standard Confucian reservation to the Emperor alone of the sacrifices to *T'ien*. See 'T'ien-t'iao shu', 73; NCH, No. 146, 163.

33. 'T'ien-ch'ao t'ien-mu chih-tu' (The land system of the Heavenly Court), TPTK, I, 321.

34. Nomura, Part II, *Kokka gakkai zasshi*, LXXII, No. 1, 321.

35. 'Tsei-ch'ing hui-tsuan', 249.

36. 'T'ai-p'ing chiu-shih-ko', 244; NCH, No. 181 (Jan. 14, 1854), 95.

37. See Chapter V, note 11.

38. Hung Jen-kan, 'Tzu-cheng hsin-p'ien' (New essay to aid in government), TPTK, II, 524.

39. 'Pan-hsing chao-shu', 161; NCH, No. 152 (June 25, 1853), 187, translates this portion of the text, but says, 'the Empire belongs to the *Chinese* [i.e. unaccountably and confusingly substitutes 'Chinese' for 'Shang-ti's'], not to the Tartars . . .'

40. 'Ch'in-ting ying-chieh kuei-chen', 592.

41. For the prospects of French monarchy after the Revolutionary era (with implications for the parody of Chinese kingship in a comparable emotional atmosphere), see the famous set of reflections on the romantic Restoration state of mind, Alfred de Musset, *La confession d'un enfant du siècle* (Paris, 1862), 10: 'Napoleon . . . destroyed and parodied the kings. . . . And after him a great noise was heard. It was the stone of St. Helena which had just fallen on the ancient world.'

42. See Fukui, 58–59, for *Chung-hsüeh* as *nei-hsüeh* in the thought of Chang Chih-t'ung, and for *nei-hsüeh* as the equivalent of *t'i* in the *t'i-yung* dichotomy.

43. Fung, II, 716; and Vol. III of the present work.

44. Cited approvingly for its Chinese application, with manual labour for cadres ensuring the (strictly non-Confucian) equality or integration of manual and intellectual work, in Li Fang, 'Cadres et Intellectuals "XIAFANG" ', *Démocratie Nouvelle* (May 1959), 43 (from editorial in *Hung-chi*, March 16, 1959).

CHAPTER IX

1. Jacob Burckhardt, *Force and Freedom* (*Weltgeschichtliche Betrachtnngen*) (New York, 1955), 181.

2. Tung Chung-shu, 1. 5a.

3. Joseph de Maistre, *Du Pape* (Paris, n.d.), 315.

4. Ojima Sukema, 'Shina shisō: shakai keizai shisō' (Chinese thought: social and economic thought), *Tōyō shichō* (Far Eastern thought-tides) (Tokyo, 1936), 23–24.

5. Hucker, 199.

6. Ch'en Shao-pai, 'Hsing Chung Hui ko-ming shih yao' (Essentials of the Hsing Chung Hui's revolutionary history), *Hsin-hai ko-ming* (Documents on the 1911 revolution) (Shanghai, 1957), I, 32.

7. Hsüeh, 19.

8. K'ang, 'Chung-kuo hsüeh-pao t'i-tz'u', 4.

9. Feng Tzu-yu, *She-hui chi-i yü Chung-kuo* (Socialism and China) (Hong Kong, 1920), 50.

10. Hu Shen-wu and Chin Ch'ung-chi, 'Hsin-hai ko-ming shih-ch'i Chang Ping-lin ti cheng-chih ssu-hsiang' (The political ideas of Chang Ping-lin at the time of the 1911 revolution), *Li-shih yen-chiu*, No. 4 (1961), 5.

11. T'ao, *Pei-yang chün-fa*, II, 112.

12. Liu Shih-p'ei, part one, CKHP, No. 1 (Jan. 1916), 3a.

13. E.g. Sun Yat-sen on Yao and Shun ('The name was monarchy, the fact was the rule of democracy'), and on Confucius and Mencius as 'pro-people's rights' on the strength of their praises of Yao and Shun; cf. Kuo Chan-po (Kōya Masao, tr.), *Gendai Shina shisō shi* (History of modern Chinese thought) (Tokyo, 1940), 108.

14. E.g. Wang Hsieh-chia, 'Chung-hua min-kuo', 2, KCWT, No. 18, for the admission that Confucianism uses heavily monarchical language—but—'What was the origin of *ko-ming*?' A 'people's rights' version of Confucianism had, of course, been worked up by K'ang Yu-wei and his Reform group, and was frequently refurbished by men like Wang, here adapting himself to the republican environment and quoting, without referring to K'ang, some of the latter's old proof-texts in the *Li-yün* section of *Li-chi*. Liu Ta-chün (see note 51, Chapter I above) does the same (KCWT, 1–2). The thinness of Confucianism in this 'republican' version is apparent, not only from its highly special selectivity but from the fact that authority has clearly been stripped from it; Confucianism, instead of dictating the polity, must be interpreted by its defenders so that it conforms to a polity established on other authority. The rhetorical question 'What is the origin of *ko-ming*?' suggests, at bottom, not that the Republic is Confucian, but that western standards have invaded even Confucianism: *Ko-ming* as revolution was from the western political vocabulary, out of Japan.

15. Cf. T'ao, *Pei-yang chün-fa*, II, 26–27, for correspondence between Ch'ing and initial Republican nomenclature. Cf. also the opinion of a dedicated republican, Liu Pai-ming, 'Kung-ho kuo-min chih ching-shen' (The spirit of a republican citizenry), *Hsüeh-heng* ('The Critical Review'), No. 10 (October 1922), 1; acknowledging disappointments, he noted that the Republic had had only ten years' trial, one three-hundredth of 'despotism's duration'. Democracy, he said, was not just a form of government, but an expression of the spirit.

16. Ch'en Huan-chang, 7a.

17. Cf. Nagano Akira, *Shina wa doku e yuku?* (Where is China going?) (Tokyo, 1927), 141-3, for a suggestion that the Chihli and Fengtien northern factions were locked in monarchical competition.

18. Tezuka, 17-19.

19. Tu Yü: see note 3, Chapter VII, above.

20. *Ming shih*, ch. 77, 4a, cited in Sohn ms.

21. Tezuka, 130. Note that the connection between *chün* and *ch'en* (and *ch'en* is located only in this or an equivalent connection) is always denoted by *lun*, human relationship; see *Li-chi*, Mencius, etc., *passim*.

22. Chang Ch'un-ming, 'Ch'ing-tai ti mu-chih' (The private-secretary system of the Ch'ing dynasty), *Lingnan hsüeh-pao*, IX, No. 2 (1950), 33-37.

23. *Ibid.* 47.

24. Sakamaki, 210.

25. *Ibid.*, 54-55.

26. T'ao, *Pei-yang chün-fa*, II, 90, 97; Jerome Ch'en, 117.

27. Sakamaki, 139.

28. Kuo Pin-chia, 'Min-kuo erh-tz'u ko-ming shih' (History of the Republic's 'Second Revolution'), part 2, *Wuhan Quarterly*, IV, No. 4 (1935), 843.

29. Sakamaki, 214-15. Sun's friend Huang Hsing, trying to win over the Ch'ing loyalist, Gen. Chang Hsün, to the anti-Yüan cause in summer, 1913, declared: 'Yüan Shih-k'ai is not only abhorrent to the Republic, he was a robber of the Ch'ing house'; cf. Kuo, part 1, *Wuhan Quarterly*, IV, No. 3, 650.

30. Li Ting-shen, *Chung-kuo chin-tai shih* (Recent history of China) (Shanghai, 1933), 312.

31. Sakamaki, 235.

32. Kuo Pin-chia, part 2, 842.

33. However, some Japanese from the most aggressive circles, ready to contemplate a take-over bid in China, not just encroachment through local action and the manipulation of blocs, opposed Yüan as emperor precisely because domestic resistance, internal disorder, seemed certain; cf. Kuzuu, 123. Perhaps it was felt that this would waste the resources which Japan might hope to attain. But this readiness for uncomplicated direct conquest was premature.

34. Kuo Pin-chia, part 1, *Wuhan Quarterly*, IV, No. 3 (1935), 637.

35. Lin Yutang, *A History of the Press and Public Opinion in China* (Chicago, 1936), 117.

36. Kuzuu, 119, 123–4, 127–30.

37. E.g. for an anti-Yüan Japanese observer's extreme scepticism about Chinese national feeling, see Sakamaki (Part 1), 277–83.

38. Tokutomi Iichirō, *Kōshaku Yamagata Aritomo den* (Biography of Prince Yamagata Aritomo) (Tokyo, 1933), III, 779, 923, 924.

39. Sanetō, 237–8.

40. K'ang, 'Chung-kuo hsüeh-pao t'i-tz'u', 6.

41. Fukui, 98.

42. Lo Chen-yü, 'Pen-chao hsüeh-shu yüan-liu kai-lueh' (General outline of the course of scholarship in the present dynasty), *Liao chü tsa-cho*, series 2, chüan 3 (Liao-tung, 1933), 1a, 2a–2b, 5b, 45a–46a.

43. For Tao, T'ien, Yao, Shun, the whole package of *wang-tao*, see Mo Shen, *Japan in Manchuria: an Analytical Study of Treaties and Documents* (Manila, 1960), 402–3; Nakayama Masaru, *Taishi seisaku no honryū* (*Nihon, Tōyō oyobi konnichi no seiki*) (The main course of policy towards China: Japan, East Asia, and the contemporary age) (Tokyo, 1937), 139–40.

44. Takata Shinji, *Shina shisō to gendai* (Chinese thought and the modern era) (Tokyo, 1940), 52, 88.

45. For education in Manchukuo as, variously, traditional and modern, see Warren W. Smith, jr., *Confucianism in Modern Japan: a Study of Conservatism in Japanese Intellectual History* (Tokyo, 1959), 187–90; F. C. Jones, *Manchuria Since 1931* (London, 1949), 46; K. K. Kawakami, *Manchukuo, Child of Conflict* (New York, 1933), 116–17.

CONCLUSION

1. Included in the draft constitution of 1908, *Hsien-fa ta-kang* (General principles of the Constitution). This was reiterated in late 1911, after the Wuchang uprising, in article one of the reform proposals of Chang Shao-tseng, the indecisive commander of the imperial Ch'ing Twentieth Division, based on Mukden; see Sakamaki, 132–3 (where the last character of the name is misprinted as 'ts'ao').

2. Ch'en Huan-chang, *K'ung-chiao lun* (On the Confucian religion) (Shanghai, 1912), 1.

3. Kita Ikki, *Shina kakumei gaishi* (Outsider's history of the Chinese revolution) (Tokyo, 1941), 22, 312–13.

4. T'ao, *Chin-tai i-wen* (Shanghai, 1930), 2; *Pei-yang chün-fa*, II, 97.

5. Heibonsha: *Seijigaku jiten* (Dictionary of political science) (Tokyo, 1957), 449.

6. *Kuo-t'i* had some vague ancient usage, as in the *Ku-liang chuan*, irrelevant to modern monarchists, and a colourless existence in occasional documents thereafter. The monarchists' *kuo-t'i* had as much novelty infused in it from Japan as the republicans' *ko-ming*.

7. Wang Shih, *Yen Fu chuan* (Biography of Yen Fu) (Shanghai, 1957), 93–94.

Bibliography

A. CHINESE AND JAPANESE

Araki Toshikazu, 'Sō-dai ni okeru denshi seiritsu no jijō' (Circumstances leading to the establishment of the palace examinations), *Tō-A jimbun gakuhō*, III, No. 2 (Oct. 1943), pp. 214–38.

Chang Ch'un-ming, 'Ch'ing-tai ti mu-chih' (The private-secretary system of the Ch'ing dynasty), *Lingnan hsüeh-pao*, IX, No. 2 (1950).

Ch'ang-t'ing, 'K'ung-hsüeh fa-wei' (The inner meaning of the Confucian learning revealed), *Chung-kuo hsüeh-pao*, No. 1 (Nov. 1912).

'Chao-shu kai-nien pan-hsing lun' (On the promulgation of imperial proclamations under fixed seal), *T'ai-p'ing T'ien-kuo* (The Heavenly Kingdom of the Great Peace), ed. Hsiang Ta et al. (Shanghai, 1952), I, pp. 301–17.

Ch'en Huan-chang, *K'ung-chiao lun* (On the Confucian religion) (Shanghai, 1912).

Ch'en Huan-chang, *K'ung-chiao lun chieh-lu* (Chapters on the Confucian religion) (Taiyuan, 1918).

Ch'en Po-ying, *Chung-kuo t'ien-chih ts'ung-k'ao* (General survey of Chinese land systems) (Shanghai, 1935).

Ch'en Shao-pai, 'Hsing Chung Hui ko-ming shih yao' (Essentials of the Hsing Chung Hui's revolutionary history), *Hsin-hai ko-ming* (Documents on the 1911 revolution) (Shanghai, 1957), I.

Ch'en Tu-hsiu, 'Hsien-fa yü K'ung-chiao' (The constitution and the Confucian religion), *Tu-hsiu wen-ts'un* (Collected essays of Ch'en Tu-hsiu) (Shanghai, 1937), pp. 103–12.

Ch'en Yin-k'o, *T'ang-tai cheng-shih shih shu-lun kao* (Draft account of T'ang political history) (Shanghai, 1947).

Ch'eng Hao, 'Lun wang pa cha-tzu' (Memorial on *wang* and *pa*), *Erh Ch'eng wen-chi* (Collection of writings of the two Ch'engs) (Chang-sha, 1941).

'Chien T'ien-ching yü Chin-ling lun' (On building the Heavenly Capital in Nanking), *T'ai-p'ing T'ien-kuo* (The Heavenly Kingdom of Great Peace), ed. Hsiang Ta et al. (Shanghai, 1952), I, pp. 249–80.

Ch'ien Mu, *Kuo-shih ta-kang* (Outline of Chinese history) (Shanghai, 1940).

'Ch'in-ting shih-chiai t'iao-li' (By imperial order: regulations for official ranks), *T'ai-p'ing T'ien-kuo* (The Heavenly Kingdom of Great Peace), ed. Hsiang Ta et al. (Shanghai, 1952), II, pp. 543–62.

'Ch'in-ting ying-chieh kuei-chen' (By imperial order: a hero returning to truth), *T'ai-p'ing T'ien-kuo* (The Heavenly Kingdom of The Great Peace), ed. Hsiang Ta et al. (Shanghai, 1952), II, pp. 563–94.

Chou Chen-fu, 'Yen Fu ssu-hsiang chuan-pien chih p'ou-hsi' (A close analysis of the changes in Yen Fu's thought), *Hsüeh-lin*, No. 3 (Jan. 1941).

Chu Shou-p'eng, ed., *Kuang-hsü Tung-hua hsü-lu* (Kuang-hsü supplement to the archival records) (Shanghai, 1908).

Feng Tzu-yu, *She-hui chu-i yü Chung-kuo* (Socialism and China) (Hong Kong, 1920).

Fukui Kōjun, *Gendai Chūgoku shisō* (Recent Chinese thought) (Tokyo, 1955).

Hara Tomio, *Chūka shisō no kontai to jugaku no yūi* (The roots of Chinese thought and the pre-eminence of Confucianism) (Tokyo, 1947).

Hattori Unokichi, *Kōshi oyobi Kōshikyō* (Confucius and the Confucian Religion) (Tokyo, 1926).

Hsia Te-wo, 'Hu-nan An-hua chiao-yü-chieh ch'üan-t'i ch'ing-ting K'ung-chiao kuo-chiao shu' (Letter from the entire educational circle of An-hua, Hunan, requesting that Confucianism be established as the state religion of China), *K'ung-chiao wen-t'i* (Problems of Confucianism), No. 17, supplement (Taiyuan, 1916).

'Hsü Chien-chieh kao-shih' (Proclamation by Hsü Chien-chieh), *T'ai-p'ing T'ien-kuo* (The Heavenly Kingdom of Great Peace), ed. Hsiang Ta et al. (Shanghai, 1952), II, pp. 892–3.

Hsüeh Cheng-ch'ing, 'K'ung-tzu kung-ho hsüeh-shuo' (The republican theory of Confucius), *Chung-kuo hsüeh-pao*, No. 7 (May, 1913).

'Hsün-t'ien Huang-ti chao' (Proclamation of the Hsün-t'ien Emperor), *T'ai-p'ing T'ien-kuo shih-liao* (Historical materials on the *T'ai-p'ing T'ien-kuo*), ed. Chin Yü-fu et al. (Peking, 1955), pp. 255–6.

Hu Shen-wu and Chin Ch'ung-chi, 'Hsin-hai ko-ming shih-ch'i Chang Ping-lin ti cheng-chih ssu-hsiang' (The political ideas of Chang Ping-lin at the time of the 1911 revolution), *Li-shih yen-chiu*, No. 4 (1961), pp. 1–20.

'Huang Wei kao-shih' (Proclamation by Huang Wei), *T'ai-p'ing T'ien-kuo* (The Heavenly Kingdom of Great Peace), ed. Hsiang Ta et al. (Shanghai, 1952), II, pp. 897–8.

Hung Jen-kan, 'Tzu-cheng hsin-p'ien' (New essay to aid in government), *T'ai-p'ing T'ien-kuo* (The Heavenly Kingdom of Great Peace), ed. Hsiang Ta et al. (Shanghai, 1952), II, pp. 522–41.

'Hu-pei kung-min Liu Ta-chün shang ts'an chung liang yüan ching ting kuo-chiao shu' (Letter from Liu Ta-chün of Hupei to the parliament requesting establishment of a state religion) *K'ung-chiao wen-t'i* (Problems of Confucianism), No. 18, supplement (Taiyuan, 1917).

BIBLIOGRAPHY

Imazeki Hisamaro, *Sung Yüan Ming Ch'ing Ju-chia hsüeh mien-piao* (Chronological tables of Sung, Yüan, Ming, and Ch'ing Confucianism) (Tokyo, 1920) (In Chinese).

Inoue Gengo, 'Juka to Haku I Tō setsuwa' (Confucianism and the tales of Po I and Tao Chih), *Shinagaku kenkyū*, No. 13 (Sept. 1955), pp. 13–22.

K'ang Yu-wei, 'Chung-kuo hsueh-hui pao t'i-tz'u' (The thesis of the journal of the Society for Chinese Learning), *Pu-jen*, II (March 1913), *chiao-shuo*, pp. 1–8.

K'ang Yu-wei, 'Chung-kuo hsüeh-pao t'i-tz'u' (The thesis of the *Chung-kuo hsüeh-pao*, No. 6 (Feb. 1913).

K'ang Yu-wei, 'Fu Chiao-yü pu shu' (Reply to the Ministry of Education), *Pu-jen*, IV (May 1913), *chiao-shuo*, pp. 1–9.

K'ang Yu-wei, 'K'ang Nan-hai chih Tsung-t'ung Tsung-li shu' (Letter from K'ang Yu-wei to the President and Premier), *K'ung-chiao wen-t'i* (Problems of Confucianism), No. 17, supplement (Taiyuan, 1916).

K'ang Yu-wei, 'K'ung-chiao hui hsü' (Preface to the Confucian Society), *Pu-jen*, I (March 1913), *Chiao-shuo*, pp. 1–10.

Kao Lao, *Ti-chih yün-tung shih-mo chi* (An account of the monarchical movement) (Shanghai, 1923).

Kita Ikki, *Shina kakumei gaishi* (Outsider's history of the Chinese Revolution) (Tokyo, 1941).

Ku Yen-wu, *Jih-chih lu* (Record of knowledge day by day) (Jui-ch'u t'ang ed., 1695).

Ku Yen-wu, *Jih-chih lu* (Record of knowledge day by day), ed. Huang Ju-ch'eng (1834).

Kuo Chan-po (Kōya Masao, tr.), *Gendai Shina shisō shi* (History of modern Chinese thought) (Tokyo, 1940).

Kuo Pin-chia, 'Min-kuo erh-tz'u ko-ming shih' (History of the Republic's 'Second Revolution'), parts one and two, *Wuhan Quarterly*, IV, Nos. 3–4 (1935).

Kuo Ting-yee, *T'ai-p'ing T'ien-kuo shih jih-chih* (Daily record of *T'ai-p'ing T'ien-kuo* historical events) (Shanghai, 1946).

Kuzuu Yoshihisa, *Nisshi kōshō gaishi* (An unofficial history of Sino-Japanese relations) (Tokyo, 1939).

Li T'ien-huai, 'Tsun K'ung shuo' (On reverence for Confucius), *Chung-kuo hsüeh-pao*, No. 7 (May 1913).

Li Ting-shen, *Chung-kuo chin-tai shih* (Recent history of China) (Shanghai, 1933).

Li Wen-chih, 'Ching ting K'ung-chiao wei kuo-chiao ti erh-tz'u i-chien shu' (Second communication of views favouring establishment of Confucianism as the state religion), *K'ung-chiao wen-t'i* (Problems of Confucianism), No. 18, supplement (Taiyuan, 1917).

Liang Ch'i-ch'ao, 'Chung-kuo chih wu-shih-tao' (China's *bushidō*), *Yin-ping-shih ho-chi* (Shanghai, 1936), ch'uan-chi 6:24, pp. 1–61.

Liu Pai-ming, 'Kung-huo kuo-min chih ching-shen' (The spirit of a republican citizenry), *Hsüeh-heng* ('The Critical Review'), No. 10 (Oct. 1922), pp. 1–6.

Liu Shih-p'ei, 'Chün-cheng fu-ku lun' (On the monarchical revival), parts one and two, *Chung-kuo hsüeh-pao*, No. 1 (Jan. 1916), No. 2 (Feb. 1916).

Lo Chen-yü, 'Pen-chao hsüeh-shu yüan-liu kai-lueh' (General outline of the course of scholarship in the present dynasty), in *Liao chü tsa-cho*, series 2, chüan 3 (Liao-tung, 1933).

Lü Ssu-mien, *Chung-kuo t'ung-shih* (General history of China) (n.p., 1941).

Miyakawa Hisayuki, 'Zenjō ni yoru ōchō kakumei no tokushitsu' (The special quality of dynastic overturns depending on 'shan-jang'), *Tōhōgaku*, No. 11 (Oct. 1955).

Miyazaki Ichisada, *Yō-sei-tei, Chūgoku no dokusai kunshu* (The Yung-cheng Emperor—China's autocratic ruler) (Tokyo, 1950).

Nagano Akira, *Shina wa doku e yuku?* (Where is China going?) (Tokyo, 1927).

Naitō Torajirō, *Shinchō shi tsūron* (Outline of Ch'ing history) (Tokyo, 1944).

Nakayama Masaru, *Taishi seisaku no honryū* (*Nihon, Tōyō oyobi konnichi no seiki*) (The main course of policy towards China: Japan, East Asia, and the contemporary age) (Tokyo, 1937).

Niida Noboru, *Chūgoku no nōson kazoku* (The Chinese peasant family) (Tokyo, 1952).

Nomura Kōichi, 'Seimatsu kōyō gakuha no keisei to Kō Yūi gaku no rekishiteki igi' (The formation of the late-Ch'ing *kung-yang* school and the historical meaning of K'ang Yu-wei's doctrine), Part One, *Kokka gakkai zasshi*, LXXI, No. 7 (1958), pp. 1–61; Part Two, *Kokka gakkai zasshi*, LXXII, No. 1, pp. 33–64.

Ojima Sukema, 'Shina shisō: shakai keizai shisō' (Chinese thought: social and economic thought), *Tōyō shichō* (Far Eastern thought-tides) (Tokyo, 1936).

'Pan-hsing chao-shu' (Proclamations published by imperial authority) *T'ai-p'ing T'ien-kuo* (The Heavenly Kingdom of Great Peace), ed. Hsiang Ta et al. (Shanghai, 1952), I, pp. 157–67.

'Pien yao-hsüeh wei tsui-li lun' (Despising the pit of fiends as durance vile), *T'ai-p'ing T'ien-kuo* (The Heavenly Kingdom of Great Peace), ed. Hsiang Ta et al. (Shanghai, 1952), I, pp. 281–99.

Rinji Taiwan kyūkan chōsakai dai-ichi-bu hōkoku (Temporary commission of the Taiwan Government-general for the study of old Chinese customs, report of the First Section), *Shinkoku gyōseihō* (Administrative laws of the Ch'ing dynasty), kan 1 (Tokyo, 1914); kan 4 (Tokyo, 1911), kan 5 (Tokyo, 1911).

Sagara Yoshiaki, 'Toku no gon no igi to sono hensen' (The meaning of the word *te* and its evolution), *Tōyō shisō kenkyū* (Studies in Far Eastern thought), No. 1, ed. Tsuda Sokichi (Tokyo, 1937).

Sakamaki Teiichirō, *Shina bunkatsu ron: tsuki, 'Gen Seikai'* (The decomposition of China: supplement, 'Yüan Shih-k'ai') (Tokyo, 1914).

BIBLIOGRAPHY

Sanetō Keishū, *Nihon bunka no Shina e no eikyō* (The influence of Japanese culture on China) (Tokyo, 1940).

Shimizu Morimitsu, 'Kyū Shina ni okeru sensei kenryoku no kiso' (The basis of autocratic power in prerevolutionary China), *Mantetsu chōsa geppō* (Bulletin of the research bureau of the South Manchuria Railway), XVII, No. 2 (Feb. 1937), pp. 1–60.

Shōji Sōichi, 'China Ryō no gaku' (The thought of Ch'en Liang), *Tōyō no bunka to shakai*, IV (1954), pp. 82–100.

Sung Yü-jen, 'K'ung-hsüeh tsung-ho cheng chiao ku chin t'ung-hsi lui pieh-lun' (On Confucianism as uniter of political and intellectual, ancient and modern systems and classes). *Chung-kuo hsüeh-pao*, No. 9 (July 1913).

Takata Shinji, *Shina shisō to gendai* (Chinese thought and the modern era) (Tokyo, 1940).

'Ta-tsung-tung kao-ling' (Presidential mandate), Sept. 25, 1914, *Chiao-yü kung-pao* (Educational record), V (June 20, 1915), *Ming-ling*, pp. 1–2.

'Ta-tsung-tung kao-ling' (Presidential mandate), Nov. 3, 1914, *Chiao-yü kung-pao* (Educational record), VII (Aug. 1915), *Ming-ling*, pp. 1–2.

'T'ai-p'ing chao-shu' (Taiping imperial proclamations), *T'ai-p'ing T'ien-kuo* (The Heavenly Kingdom of Great Peace), ed. Hsiang Ta et al. (Shanghai, 1952), I, pp. 85–99.

'T'ai-p'ing chiu-shih-ko' (Taiping songs on salvation), *T'ai-p'ing T'ien-kuo* (The Heavenly Kingdom of the Great Peace), ed. Hsiang Ta et al. (Shanghai, 1952), I, pp. 237–47.

'T'ai-p'ing t'ien-jih' (Taiping days), *T'ai-p'ing T'ien-kuo* (The Heavenly Kingdom of Great Peace), ed. Hsiang Ta et al. (Shanghai, 1952), II, pp. 629–50.

T'ao Chü-yin, *Chin-tai i-wen* (Items about the modern era) (Shanghai, 1940).

T'ao Chü-yin, *Liu chün-tzu chuan* (Biographies of the 'Six Martyrs') (Shanghai, 1946).

T'ao Chü-yin, *Pei-yang chün-fa t'ung-chih shih-ch'i shih-hua* (Historical discourses on the era of the Pei-yang military clique's dominion), Vols. 1–4 (Peking, 1957); Vol. 5 (Peking, 1958).

Tezuka Ryōdō, *Jukyō dōtoku ni okeru kunshin shisō* (The sovereign-minister idea in Confucian ethics) (Tokyo, 1925).

'T'ien-ch'ao t'ien-mu chih-tu' (The land system of the Heavenly Court), *T'ai-p'ing T'ien-kuo* (The Heavenly Kingdom of the Great Peace), ed. Hsiang Ta et al. (Shanghai, 1952), I, pp. 319–26.

'T'ien-ch'ing tao-li shu' (Book of the divine nature and principles), *T'ai-p'ing T'ien-kuo* (The Heavenly Kingdom of the Great Peace), ed. Hsiang Ta et al. (Shanghai, 1952), I, pp. 353–406.

'T'ien-fu hsia-fan chao-shu' (Book of declarations of the divine will made during the Heavenly Father's descent upon earth), *T'ai-p'ing t'ien-kuo* (The Heavenly Kingdom of the Great Peace), ed. Hsiang Ta et al. (Shanghai, 1952), I, pp. 7–20.

BIBLIOGRAPHY

'T'ien-lu yao-lun' (On the essentials of the principles of heaven), *T'ai-p'ing T'ien-kuo* (The Heavenly Kingdom of the Great Peace), ed. Hsiang Ta et al. (Shanghai, 1952), I, pp. 327–52.

'T'ien-ming chao-chih-shu' (Book of heavenly decrees and imperial edicts), *T'ai-p'ing T'ien-kuo* (The Heavenly Kingdom of Great Peace), ed. Hsiang Ta et al. (Shanghai, 1952), pp. 5–70.

'T'ien-te Wang t'ieh Liu-chou kao-shih' (Proclamation of T'ien-te Wang affixed at Liu-chou) (The Heavenly Kingdom of Great Peace), ed. Hsiang Ta et al. (Shanghai, 1952), II, pp. 891–2.

'T'ien-ti hui chao-shu' (Decree of the *T'ien-ti hui*), *T'ai-p'ing T'ien-kuo shih-liao* (Historical materials on the *T'ai-p'ing T'ien-kuo*), ed. Chin Yü-fu et al. (Peking, 1955), pp. 256–7.

'T'ien-t'iao shu' (Book of the laws of Heaven), *T'ai-p'ing T'ien-kuo* (The Heavenly Kingdom of the Great Peace), ed. Hsiang Ta et al. (Shanghai, 1952), I, pp. 71–83.

Toda Toyosaburō, 'Gogyō setsu seiritsu no ichi kōsatsu' (Reflection on the formation of five-element theory), *Shinagaku kenkyū*, XII (1956), pp. 38–45.

Tokutomi Iichirō, *Kōshaku Yamagata Aritomo den* (Biography of Prince Yamagata Aritomo), Vol. III (Tokyo, 1933).

'Tsei-ch'ing hui-tsuan' (Collected materials on the circumstances of the thieves) *T'ai-p'ing T'ien-kuo* (The Heavenly Kingdom of the Great Peace), ed. Hsiang Ta et al. (Shanghai, 1952), III, pp. 23–348.

Tso Shun-sheng, *Wan-chu lou sui-pi* (Sketches from the Wan-chü chamber) (Hong Kong, 1953).

Tu Erh-wei, *Chung-kuo ku-tai tsung-chiao yen-chiu* (Studies on the ancient religions of China) (Taipei, 1959).

Tung Chung-shu, *Ch'un-ch'iu fan-lu* (Luxuriant dew from the *Spring and Autumn Annals*) (Shanghai, 1929).

Wang Hsieh-chia, 'Chung-hua min-kuo hsien-fa hsüan ch'uan chang ting K'ung-chiao wei kuo-chiao ping hsü jen-min hsiu chiao tzu-yu hsiu-cheng an' (Proposal that the constitution of the Republic of China promulgate a special clause establishing Confucianism as the state religion and permitting modification of the freedom of religion), *K'ung-chiao wen-t'i* (Problems of Confucianism), No. 18, supplement (Taiyuan, 1917).

Wang Shih, *Yen Fu chuan* (Biography of Yen Fu) (Shanghai, 1957).

Wei Yüan, *Ku-wei t'ang chi*, 1878 (Huai-nan shu-chü ed.).

Wu Li, 'K'ung-tzu fei Man-chou chih fu-hu' (Let Confucius not be an amulet for the Manchu), *Min-pao*, No. 11 (Jan. 30, 1907).

'Yang Hsiu-ch'ing Hsiao Ch'ao-kuei hui-hsien kao-yü' (Joint proclamation of Yang Hsiu-ch'ing and Hsiao Ch'ao-kuei), *T'ai-p'ing T'ien-kuo* (The Heavenly Kingdom of the Great Peace), ed. Hsiang Ta et al. (Shanghai, 1952), II, pp. 691–2.

Yang Yin-shen, *Chung-kuo wen-hsüeh-chia lieh-chuan* (Biographies of Chinese literary figures) (Shanghai, 1939).

Yang Yu-ch'iung, *Chung-kuo cheng-chih ssu-shiang shih* (History of Chinese political thought) (Shanghai, 1937).

Yang Yu-ch'iung (Moriyama Takashi, tr.), *Shina seitō shi* (History of Chinese political parties) (Tokyo, 1940).

B. WESTERN

Alföldi, Andrew, *A Conflict of Ideas in the Late Roman Empire: the Clash between the Senate and Valentinian I* (Oxford, 1952).

Barber, Elinor G., *The Bourgeoisie in 18th century France* (Princeton, 1955).

Barbu, Zevedei, *Problems of Historical Psychology* (New York, 1960).

Baron, Salo Wittmayer, *A Social and Religious History of the Jews*, Volume One (New York, 1952).

Baynes, Norman H., *Byzantine Studies and Other Essays* (London, 1955).

Bernard-Maitre, Henri, *Sagesse chinoise et philosophie chrétienne* (Paris, 1935).

Bloch, Marc, *Les rois thaumaturges* (Strasbourg, 1924).

Boardman, Eugene Powers, *Christian Influence Upon the Ideology of the Taiping Rebellion, 1851–1864* (Madison, 1952).

Brewitt-Taylor, C. H., tr., *The Romance of the Three Kingdoms* (Shanghai, 1925).

Brogan, D. W., 'The "Nouvelle Revue Française" ', *Encounter* (March 1959), pp. 66–68.

Bruford, W. H., 'The Idea of "Bildung" in Wilhelm von Humboldt's Letters', *The Era of Goethe: Essays Presented to James Boyd* (Oxford, 1959), pp. 17–46.

Burckhardt, Jacob, *Force and Freedom* (*Weltgeschichtliche Betrachtungen*) (New York, 1955).

Cahill, James F., 'Confucian Elements in the Theory of Painting', *The Confucian Persuasion*, ed. Arthur F. Wright (Stanford, 1960), pp. 115–40.

Chan, David, 'The Problem of the Princes As Faced by the Ming Emperor Hui (1399–1402)', *Oriens*, XI, Nos. 1–2 (1958), pp. 183–93.

Chan, David B., 'The Role of the Monk Tao-Yen in the Usurpation of the Prince of Yen (1398–1402)', *Sinologica*, VI, No. 2 (1959), pp. 83–100.

Chang, Carsun, *The Development of Neo-Confucian Thought* (New York, 1957).

Chang Jen-hsia, 'Flower-and-Bird Painting', *China Reconstructs*, III (May–June 1953).

Chao Yuen Ren, 'What is Correct Chinese?' *Journal of the American Oriental Society*, LXXXI, No. 3 (Aug.–Sept. 1961), pp. 171–7.

Ch'en, Jerome, *Yuan Shih-k'ai (1859–1916): Brutus assumes the Purple* (London, 1961).

Cherniavsky, Michael, *Tsar and People: Studies in Russian Myths* (New Haven and London, 1961).

BIBLIOGRAPHY

Chow Tse-tsung, 'The Anti-Confucian Movement in Early Republican China', *The Confucian Persuasion*, ed. Arthur F. Wright (Stanford, 1960).

Cobban, Alfred, *A History of Modern France: Volume One, Old Régime and Revolution, 1715-1799* (Harmondsworth, 1957).

Cohn, Norman, *The Pursuit of the Millennium* (London, 1957).

Dakin, Douglas, *Turgot and the Ancien Régime in France* (London, 1939).

d'Avenel, G., *La noblesse française sous Richelieu* (Paris, 1901).

de Bary, W. Theodore, 'A Reappraisal of Neo-Confucianism', *Studies in Chinese Thought*, ed. Arthur F. Wright (Chicago, 1953), pp. 81–111.

de Bary, W. T., 'Chinese Despotism and the Confucian Ideal: A Seventeenth-Century View', *Chinese Thought and Institutions*, ed. John K. Fairbank (Chicago, 1957), pp. 163–203.

Delatte, Louis, *Les traités de la royauté d'Ecphante, Diotegène, et Sthénidas* (Liege and Paris, 1942).

de Maistre, Joseph, *Du Pape* (Paris, n.d.).

De Musset, Alfred, *La confession d'un enfant du siècle* (Paris, 1862).

des Rotours, Robert, *Le traité des examens, traduit de la Nouvelle histoire des T'ang* (Paris, 1932).

de Tocqueville, Alexis, *The Old Régime and the French Revolution* (New York, 1955).

Diderot, Denis, 'The Encyclopaedia', *'Rameau's Nephew' and Other Works*, tr. Jacques Barzun and Ralph H. Bowen (New York, 1956), pp. 291–323.

Duyvendak, J. J. L., *China's Discovery of Africa* (London, 1949).

Fallers, L. A., 'Despotism, Status Culture and Social Mobility in an African Kingdom', *Comparative Studies in Society and History*, II, No. 1 (Oct. 1959), pp. 11–32.

Febvre, Lucien, *Au coeur religieux du XVIe siècle* (Paris, 1957).

Ferrero, Guglielmo, *The Principles of Power* (New York, 1942).

Ford, Franklin L., *Robe and Sword: the Regrouping of the French Aristocracy after Louis XIV* (Cambridge, Mass., 1953).

Franke, Wolfgang, *The Reform and Abolition of the Traditional Chinese Examination System* (Cambridge, Mass., 1960).

Freedman, Maurice, *Lineage Organization in Southeastern China* (London, 1958).

Freedman, Maurice, 'The Family in China, Past and Present', *Pacific Affairs*, XXXIV, No. 4 (Winter 1961–2), pp. 323–36.

Fung Yu-lan, *A History of Chinese Philosophy: the Period of the Philosophers* (from the Beginnings to *circa* 100 B.C.), tr. Derk Bodde (Peiping, 1937).

Fung Yu-lan, *A History of Chinese Philosophy: Volume Two, The Period of Classical Learning*, tr. Derk Bodde (Princeton, 1953).

Gay, Peter, *Voltaire's Politics: the Poet as Realist* (Princeton, 1959).

Gernet, Jacques, *Daily Life in China on the Eve of the Mongol Invasion 1250–1276* (New York, 1962).

BIBLIOGRAPHY

Gernet, Jacques, *Les aspects économiques du Bouddhisme dans la société chinoise du Ve au Xe siècle* (Saigon, 1956).

Grant, Michael, *From Imperium to Auctoritas: a Historical Study of Aes Coinage in the Roman Empire, 49 B.C.–A.D. 14* (Cambridge, 1946).

Griggs, Thurston, 'The Ch'ing Shih Kao: a Bibliographical Summary', *Harvard Journal of Asiatic Studies*, XVIII, Nos. 1–2 (June 1955), pp. 105–23.

Hadas, Moses, *Hellenistic Culture: Fusion and Diffusion* (New York, 1959).

Hanotaux, Gabriel, and Le Duc de la Force, *Histoire du Cardinal de Richelieu* (Paris, 1899).

Heibonsha: *Seijigaku jiten* (Dictionary of political science) (Tokyo, 1957).

Herr, Richard, *Tocqueville and the Old Régime* (Princeton, 1962).

Hintze, Otto, *Staat und Verfassung* (Leipzig, 1941).

Ho Ping-ti, 'Aspects of Social Mobility in China, 1368–1911', *Comparative Studies in Society and History*, I, 4 (June 1959), pp. 330–59.

Ho Ping-ti, *Studies on the Population of China, 1368–1953* (Cambridge, Mass., 1959).

Houn, Franklin W., *Central Government in China: an Institutional Study* (Madison, 1957).

Hsiao Kung-chuan, *Rural China: Imperial Control in the Nineteenth Century* (Seattle, 1960).

Hu, C. T., 'The Ning Wang Revolt: Sociology of a Ming Rebellion' (Association for Asian Studies, ms., 1959).

Huang Sung-K'ang, *Lu Hsün and the New Culture Movement of Modern China* (Amsterdam, 1957).

Hucker, Charles O., 'Confucianism and the Chinese Censorial System', *Confucianism in Action*, ed. David S. Nivison and Arthur F. Wright (Stanford, 1959), pp. 182–208.

Hurvitz, Leon, ' "Render unto Caesar" in Early Chinese Buddhism', *Sino-Indian Studies: Liebenthal Festschrift*, ed. Kshitis Roy (Visvabharati, 1957), pp. 80–114.

Jones, F. C., *Manchuria Since 1931* (London, 1949).

Jones, J. Walter, *The Law and Legal Theory of the Greeks* (Oxford, 1956).

Kantorowicz, Ernst, *Frederick the Second, 1194–1250* (London, 1931).

Kantorowicz, Ernst H., *Laudes Regiae: A Study in Liturgical Acclamations and Mediaeval Ruler Worship* (Berkeley and Los Angeles, 1946).

Kantorowicz, Ernst H., *The King's Two Bodies: a study in Mediaeval Political Theology* (Princeton, 1957).

Kaufmann, Walter, *Nietzsche* (New York, 1956).

Kawakami, K. K., *Manchukuo, Child of Conflict* (New York, 1933).

Kraus, Wolfgang H., 'Authority, Progress, and Colonialism', *Nomos I: Authority*, ed. Carl J. Friedrich (Cambridge, 1958), pp. 145–56.

Krieger, Leonard, *The German Idea of Freedom: History of a Political Tradition* (Boston, 1957).

Lefebvre, Georges, *Etudes sur la Revolution française* (Paris, 1954).

Lefebvre, Georges, *The Coming of the French Revolution, 1789* (Princeton, 1947).

Legge, James, tr., *The Li Ki*, Books I–X, *Sacred Books of the East*, ed. F. Max Muller (Oxford, 1885).

Levenson, Joseph R., 'Ill Wind in the Well-Field: The Erosion of the Confucian Ground of Controversy', *The Confucian Persuasion*, ed. Arthur F. Wright (Stanford, 1960), pp. 268–87.

Levy, Howard S., *Biography of An Lu-shan* (Berkeley and Los Angeles, 1960).

Levy, Howard S., *Biography of Huang Ch'ao* (Berkeley and Los Angeles, 1955).

Lewis, Ewart, *Medieval Political Ideas* (New York, 1954).

Li Fang, 'Cadres et Intellectuels "XIAFANG" ', *Démocratie Nouvelle* (May 1959), pp. 43–44.

Liao, Joshua, 'The Empire Breaker', *The Orient*, 10 (May 1951).

Lin Yutang, *A History of the Press and Public Opinion in China* (Chicago, 1936).

Liu, Hui-chen Wang, 'An Analysis of Chinese Clan Rules: Confucian Theories in Action', *Confucianism in Action*, ed. David S. Nivison and Arthur F. Wright (Stanford, 1959), pp. 63–96.

✓ Liu, James T. C., 'Some Classifications of Bureaucrats in Chinese Historiography', *Confucianism in Action*, ed. David S. Nivison and Arthur F. Wright (Stanford, 1959), pp. 165–81.

MacSherry, Charles Whitman, *Impairment of the Ming Tributary System as Exhibited in Trade Involving Fukien* (dissertation, University of California, 1957).

Maimonides, Moses, *Guide of the Perplexed*, tr. M. Friedländer (New York, n.d.).

Mancall, Mark, 'China's First Missions to Russia, 1729–1731', *Papers on China*, IX (Harvard University, August 1955), pp. 75–110.

Mann, Thomas, *Doctor Faustus* (New York, 1948).

Marmorstein, A., *The Old Rabbinic Doctrine of God* (London, 1927).

Marsh, Robert M., 'Bureaucratic Constraints on Nepotism in the Ch'ing Period', *Journal of Asian Studies*, XIX, No. 2 (Feb. 1960), pp. 117–33.

Marx, Fritz Morstein, *The Administrative State: an Introduction to Bureaucracy* (Chicago, 1957).

Maspéro, Henri, 'Comment tombe une dynastie chinoise: la chute des Ming', *Etudes historiques* (Paris, 1950).

Mayers, William Frederick, *The Chinese Government* (Shanghai, 1886).

Mo Shen, *Japan in Manchuria: an Analytical Study of Treaties and Documents* (Manila, 1960).

Montesquieu, *The Spirit of the Laws*, tr. Thomas Nugent (New York, 1949).

Mote, Frederick W., 'Confucian Eremitism in the Yüan Period', *The Confucian Persuasion*, ed. Arthur F. Wright (Stanford, 1960), pp. 202–40.

Neumann, Franz, 'Montesquieu', *The Democratic and the Authoritarian State: Essays in Political and Legal Theory* (Glencoe, III, 1957), pp. 96–148.

Nivison, David S., 'Ho-shen and His Accusers: Ideology and Political Behavior in the Eighteenth Century', *Confucianism in Action*, ed. David S. Nivison and Arthur F. Wright (Stanford, 1959), pp. 209–43.

North China Herald, Shanghai.

Norton, Lucy, tr. *Saint-Simon at Versailles* (New York, 1958).

Orwell, George, *The English People* (London, 1947).

Palmer, R. R., 'Georges Lefebvre: the Peasants and the French Revolution', *Journal of Modern History*, XXXI, No. 4 (Dec. 1959), pp. 329–42.

Pan Ku, *The History of the Former Han Dynasty*, Vol. II, tr. Homer H. Dubs (Baltimore, 1944).

'Passing Events in China (from Dr. D. J. Macgowan's Note Book)', *North-China Herald*, No. 159 (Aug. 13, 1853), p. 7.

'Proclamation of One of the Insurgent Chiefs', *North-China Herald*, No. 137 (March 12, 1853), pp. 126–7.

Pulleyblank, Edwin G., 'Neo-Confucianism and Neo-Legalism in T'ang Intellectual Life, 755–805', *The Confucian Persuasion*, ed. Arthur F. Wright (Stanford, 1960), pp. 77–114.

Pulleyblank, Edwin G., *The Background of the Rebellion of An Lu-shan* (London, New York, and Toronto, 1955).

Rosenberg, Hans, *Bureaucracy, Aristocracy, and Autocracy: the Prussian Experience, 1660–1815* (Cambridge, Mass., 1958).

Rosenthal, Erwin I. J., *Political Thought in Medieval Islam: an Introductory Outline* (Cambridge, 1958).

Rosenthal, E. I. J., 'Some Aspects of the Hebrew Monarchy', *The Journal of Jewish Studies*, IX, Nos. 1 and 2 (1958), pp. 1–18.

Rude, George, *The Crowd in the French Revolution* (Oxford, 1959).

Schumpeter, Joseph, 'The Sociology of Imperialism', *'Imperialism' and 'Social Classes'* (New York, 1955), pp. 1–98.

✓ Schwartz, Benjamin, 'Some Polarities in Confucian Thought', *Confucianism in Action*, ed. David S. Nivison and Arthur F. Wright (Stanford, 1959), pp. 50–63.

Shih, Vincent, *The Ideology of the T'ai-p'ing T'ien-kuo* (University of Washington, ms.).

Sinnigen, William Gurnee, *The Officium of the Urban Prefecture During the Later Roman Empire* (Rome, 1957).

Sinnigen, William G., 'The Vicarius Urbis Romae and the Urban Prefecture', *Historia*, VIII, No. 1 (Jan. 1959), pp. 97–112.

Smith, Warren W., jr., *Confucianism in Modern Japan: A Study of Conservatism in Japanese Intellectual History* (Tokyo, 1959).

Sohn, Pow-key, 'The Theory and Practice of Land-systems in Korea in Comparison with China' (University of California, ms., 1956).

Soper, Alexander, 'Standards of Quality in Northern Sung Painting', *Archives of the Chinese Art Society of America*, XI (1957), pp. 8–15.

Strayer, Joseph R., 'Feudalism in Western Europe', *Feudalism in History*, ed. Rushton Coulborn (Princeton, 1956), pp. 15–25.

BIBLIOGRAPHY

Taine, Hippolyte Adolphe, *The Ancient Régime* (New York, 1931).

Teng Ssu-yü, 'Hung Hsiu-ch'üan', *Eminent Chinese of the Ch'ing Period*, ed. Arthur W. Hummel (Washington, 1943), I, pp. 361–7.

'The Book of Celestial Decrees and Declarations of the Imperial Will', *North-China Herald*, No. 148 (May 28, 1853), p. 172.

'The Book of Religious Precepts of the T''hae-ping Dynasty', *North-China Herald*, No. 146 (May 14, 1853), p. 163.

Twitchett, Denis, 'The Fan Clan's Charitable Estate, 1050–1760', *Confucianism in Action*, ed. David S. Nivison and Arthur F. Wright (Stanford, 1959), pp. 97–133.

van Gulik, R. H., tr., *T'ang-Yun-Pi-Shih*, '*Parallel Cases from under the Pear-Tree*' (Leiden, 1956).

Vernadsky, George, *A History of Russia* (New Haven, 1951).

Waley, Arthur, *Yuan Mei, Eighteenth Century Chinese Poet* (New York, 1956).

Watkins, J. W. N., 'Milton's Vision of a Reformed England', *The Listener*, LXI, No. 1556 (Jan. 22, 1959), pp. 168–9, 172.

Watson, Burton, *Ssu-ma Ch'ien, Grand Historian of China* (New York, 1958).

Weber, Max, 'Politics As a Vocation', *From Max Weber: Essays in Sociology*, ed. H. H. Gerth and C. Wright Mills (New York, 1946), pp. 77–128.

Wittfogel, Karl A., *Oriental Despotism: A Comparative Study of Total Power* (New Haven, 1957).

Wittfogel, Karl A., and Feng Chia-sheng, *History of Chinese Society: Liao* (907–1125) (Philadelphia, 1949).

Wolff, Robert Lee, 'The Three Romes: the Migration of an Ideology and the Making of an Autocrat', *Daedalus* (Spring 1959), pp. 291–311.

Wolfson, Harry Austryn, *Philo: Foundations of Religious Philosophy in Judaism, Christianity and Islam* (Cambridge, Mass., 1947).

Wright, Arthur F., 'Sui Yang-ti: Personality and Stereotype', *The Confucian Persuasion*, pp. 47–76.

Yang Lien-sheng, 'Notes on Dr. Swann's "Food and Money in Ancient China" ', *Studies in Chinese Institutional History* (Cambridge, Mass., 1961), pp. 85–118.

Zürcher, E., *The Buddhist Conquest of China: the Spread and Adaptation of Buddhism in Early Medieval China* (Leiden, 1959).

Index

INDEX